THE ROCKIES

Storm clouds in Amethyst Basin, High Uintas, Utah.

Paradise Basin, San Juan Mountains, Colorado.

Big Thompson River, Rocky Mountain National Park, Colorado; (right) pond in San Juan Mountains, Colorado.

THE ROCKIES

Backbone of a Continent

Willard Clay

WRITTEN BY JEREMY SCHMIDT
PRODUCED BY McQUISTON & PARTNERS

THUNDER BAY PRESS, SAN DIEGO

Willard Clay

A spen leaves turning gold are
the symbol of autumn in the
Rockies—in many ways the
most beautiful of the seasons.
It is a time when the bugling
of bull elk echoes among the
chilly peaks, frost hardens
the ground overnight, and
snow can fall at any
moment.

Producing a book on a subject as large and diverse as the Rocky Mountains is a formidable undertaking. So we felt fortunate in being able to assemble a creative team that cut the task down to size. Writer Jeremy Schmidt proved to have an even greater knowledge of the Mountain West than we had imagined. He also shot some of the photographs that appear in the book, although most of the 150 superb color images came from other talented camera people: Jim Brandenburg, Kathy and Willard Clay, W. Perry Conway, Jeff Gnass, Tom and Pat Leeson, Pat Morrow, Pat O'Hara, David Stoecklein, Tom Till, and Larry Ulrich. We are also grateful to Bob Volpert of Outdoor Adventures in Point Reyes Station, California, who generously provided space on the Salmon River trip described in Part Two. Finally, to Charles Tillinghast and Craig Schafer of Thunder Bay Press—thanks for another great opportunity.

—McQuiston & Partners

To my grandfather, who never got lost in the woods.

Library of Congress Cataloging-in-Publication Data:
Schmidt, Jeremy, 1949-
    The Rockies: backbone of a continent/written by
    Jeremy Schmidt.
        p.   cm.
    Bibliography: p.
    Includes index.
    1. Rocky Mountains. 2. Natural history—Rocky
    Mountains.
I. Title.
F721.S343   1990   917.8—dc20   89-80489 CIP
ISBN 0-934429-19-7
10 9 8 7 6 5 4 3 2 1

Photo Credits
Cover: Mistaya River Area, Banff, Alberta by
Pat O'Hara

Printed in Japan by Dai Nippon Printing Co., Ltd.

Published by Thunder Bay Press
5880 Oberlin Drive
San Diego, CA 92121

CONTENTS

Tom Till

Early snowstorm on Mount Timpanogos, Utah.

INTRODUCTION
THE SHINING MOUNTAINS

Wyoming Highway 191 can be a long and lonely road. In December, on a snowy day, the pavement rolls along mile after mile. Clouds hang low. The wind blows hard; it always blows hard in the middle of Wyoming. It pushes snow across the open sage. It builds drifts that finger their way onto the pavement, grabbing at car tires.

If there hasn't been a vehicle on the road for a while, drifts get big enough that when you hit them, a billow of snow comes over the windshield and for a few seconds you can't see anything but white, as if you've hit a wave on a surfboard. Every so often, you notice secondary roads headed into that sea of white. At the town of Farson, Highway 28 goes east. It eventually reaches Lander, but that's nearly 80 miles away across one of the emptiest places in the Lower Forty-eight.

Winter in south-central Wyoming. It's hard to believe that this great openness is in the middle of the Rocky Mountains. Out here, it's hard to believe in much besides your car heater.

I remember reading in the papers, ten or fifteen years ago, about a young man who was found on one of those lonely Wyoming roads. He was a traveler, passing through, by himself. His car broke down on a winter day. He waited, I recall, about eight hours. When no one drove past in that time, he despaired. He wrote a note. He shot himself. It seems the country was just too much for him.

Maybe he read the same book I did. It claimed that this region contains the "world's largest body of shifting sand and desert land—about 700 square miles." That seems impossible when you consider the Sahara, the Sinai, and the Takla Makan (China) deserts. I can't vouch for the claim, but I know that the dunes do stretch for more than a hundred miles, west to east. If you dig down a few inches in the sandy hollows, you can find water—sometimes ice. Even in summer, there is ice under the hot sand.

This is the Great Divide Basin, named for its location within the Continental Divide—the delineator of the North American watershed. To the west is the Pacific Ocean; to the east, the Atlantic. Generally speaking the Divide follows the crest of the Rocky Mountains, all the way from northern Canada to the middle of New Mexico. For most of that distance, it stays high and purposeful. But in Wyoming, south of the Wind River Range, it performs this stunt: It forks to enclose the Great Divide Basin, a big sandy bowl filled with sagebrush and air, where water flows neither to the Atlantic nor to the Pacific. And there is not a mountain in sight.

Strange stories about a strange territory, and only one of many surprises in the Rocky Mountain region. There is a place in Yellowstone where the east side of the Divide faces west. In New Mexico, there is a little-known valley in the shape of a circle.

Entire rivers disappear beneath the lava plains of south-central Idaho. Every fall in Glacier National Park, there is a salmon run made by fish that have never seen the ocean. Also in Glacier Park, an impressive matterhorn called Chief Mountain is made of rock far older than the rock upon which it stands. How could that happen? And how is it that we find petrified redwood trees in Yellowstone National Park? Or the delicate remains of tsetse flies at Florissant Fossil Beds National Monument?

It is a truism: All mountains seen from a distance appear simple in structure, but close up they become enormously complicated. For the Rockies, this is especially true if you see them from the east, from out across the rolling plains of Colorado, Montana, or Alberta. They rise like a shining wall just over the horizon, a bold, unified gesture gleaming under the big western sky.

Seeing them that way, from the plains, you can easily imagine the Rockies shouldering their way up from an ancient seafloor some 70 million years ago. It was a dramatic event in the history of North America. After some 400 million years of quiet on the geologic front, things began to stir. The continent was drifting west, pulling away from Europe. As it moved, it pushed against and over the floor of the Pacific Ocean. That movement disturbed the semimolten layer beneath the earth's crust, causing havoc on the surface. The land was elevated, stretched, and broken.

That period of change, called the Laramide Orogeny or uplift, marked the birth of the Rockies. But it was only the beginning of what we see today.

As soon as the land rose above sea level, erosive forces—wind, water, and ice—began wearing it down. Then volcanoes erupted, building new mountain ranges, further complicating the story. There was more uplift, more erosion, more volcanic activity.

During this time, the western part of the continent witnessed some of the most violent geologic events ever known to have occurred. In places, vast islands of rock were pushed up while neighboring rocks fell. Volcanic eruptions covered huge areas of land, building new mountains. Glaciers blocked entire valleys. The enormous lakes that built up behind the ice periodically emptied, causing science-fiction-type floods.

If there's one lesson to be learned from geology, it is the lesson of impermanence. The earth moves and nothing, not even a mountain range, is eternal. I have a friend, a geologist who studies Yellowstone. After the 1988 forest fires burned over 1 million acres, he said, in all seriousness, "Mind you, only the tiniest fraction of the park has burned. There are seven or eight thousand feet of geology, between the surface and sea level, that haven't been touched."

I have to admit, his observation had a certain grim validity. More than once in the recent geologic past, Yellowstone has been destroyed. The area has experienced a series of mind-boggling volcanic catastrophes. The most recent was about 600,000 years ago. There is evidence that similar events occurred around 1.2 and 1.8 million years ago, and they may have been happening long before that.

Each time, the region now called Yellowstone suddenly exploded. Molten rock, building pressure beneath the surface, became too great for the overlying rock to contain. The resulting eruptions were enormous. In the most recent one, some 100 cubic miles of debris were hurled into the sky in a matter of hours. Windrows of Yellowstone ash several feet deep have been found as far east as Kansas.

All that was left in Yellowstone was a smoking crater measuring roughly 30 by 60 miles. In comparison, the eruption of Mount St. Helens was a minor event. And so were the forest fires of 1988.

The Rocky Mountains stretch from New Mexico almost to Canada's Yukon Territory—2,000 miles and 25 degrees of latitude, the same as Sicily to Stockholm or Atlanta to Greenland.

Their width varies. In Canada, they are relatively narrow, involving one or two major lines of high peaks along the Continental Divide. In the United States, they expand to include numerous subranges, reaching their widest point at about 45 degrees latitude—the northern boundary of Wyoming. They stay wide and complex all the way to southern Colorado and then narrow down again to just two sharp crests extending into New Mexico. Their southern end is near Santa Fe.

When trying to get a feel for this massive, complicated piece of country, it makes sense to divide the range into three regions—south, middle, and north. Each region has distinctive characteristics of geology, topography, plant and animal life, his-

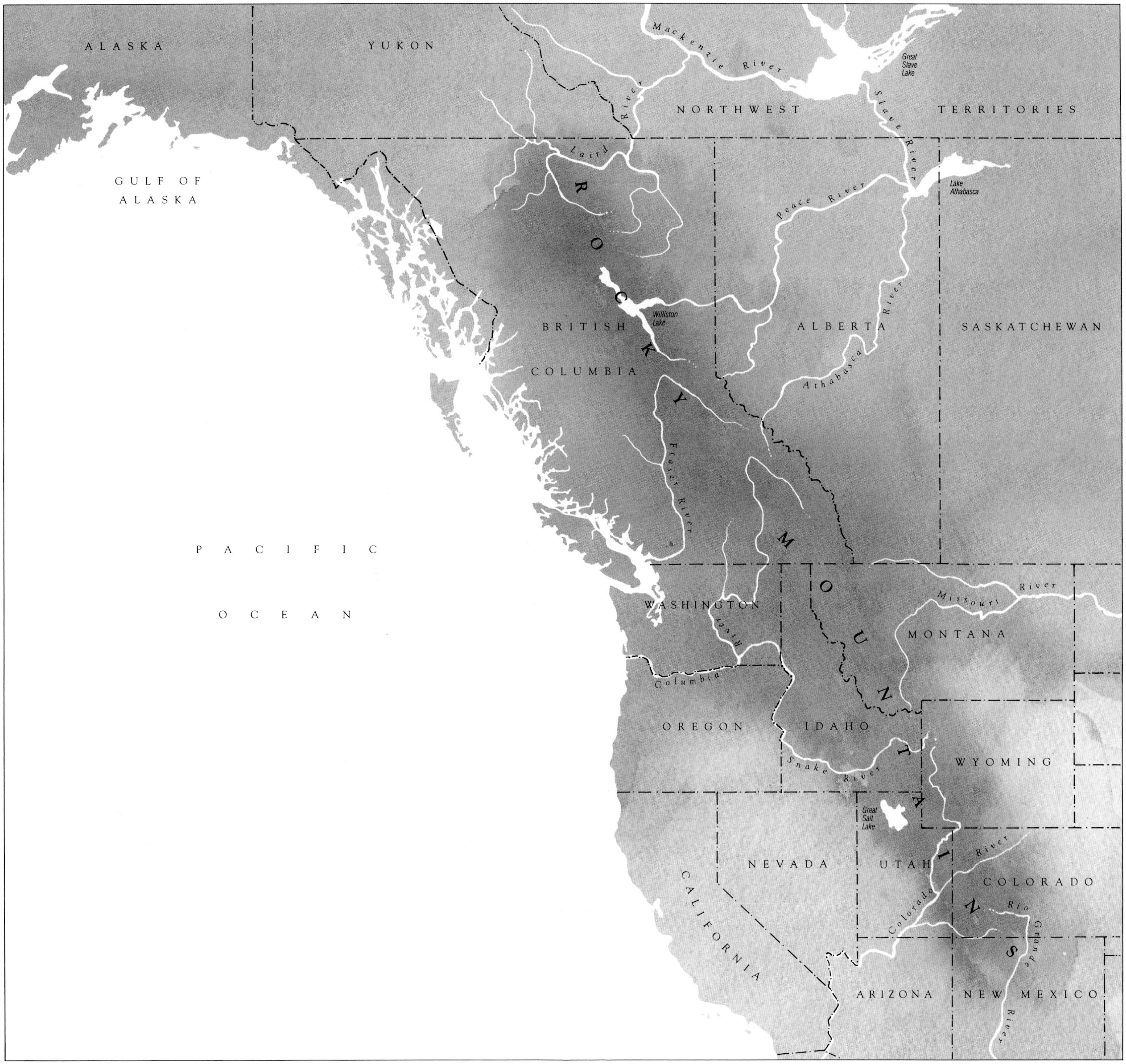

ALASKA

YUKON

NORTHWEST   TERRITORIES

Mackenzie River

Great Slave Lake

GULF OF ALASKA

Liard River

R O C K Y

Peace River

Slave River

Lake Athabasca

BRITISH

Williston Lake

ALBERTA   SASKATCHEWAN

COLUMBIA

Athabasca River

Fraser River

P A C I F I C

M O U N T A I N S

Missouri River

O C E A N

WASHINGTON

MONTANA

Columbia River

O   IDAHO

OREGON

Snake River

WYOMING

Great Salt Lake

River

NEVADA   UTAH

COLORADO

Colorado River

CALIFORNIA

Rio Grande

ARIZONA   NEW MEXICO

River

tory, and culture. The southern Rockies are essentially the Colorado Rockies, reaching south into New Mexico and north a few miles into Wyoming. The highest peaks in the range (the only ones over 14,000 feet) are found here, giving rise to the great desert rivers of the Southwest, the Rio Grande and the Colorado. The middle Rockies occupy northern Wyoming, central Idaho, and parts of Montana, an area dominated by geologic instability. Volcanoes were active in the region as recently as 60,000 years ago; geologists tell us that places like Yellowstone could erupt at any time. Finally, the northern Rockies begin around Helena, Montana and extend all the way to northern British Columbia before fading into subarctic forest. The northern Rockies are composed mostly of sedimentary rock, which imparts a sense of ponderous bulk to the mountains; they are lower than the peaks of Colorado, but they *seem* bigger.

There are other ranges in British Columbia immediately to the west of the Rockies. On a map, these mountains seem to be part of the same geography, but they are not. They are older than the Rockies; they are made of different rock; and they are separated from the Rockies by a major geologic fault line, the Rocky Mountain Trench. From the geologic point of view, these other ranges—the Selkirks, the Purcells, the Monashees, and the Cariboos, collectively called the Columbia Mountains—occupy a whole different country. To tell a geologist that the distinction is unimportant is like telling a man in Wales that he lives in England. The notion is preposterous. On the other hand, they are close neighbors. Just as Canada borders the United States, the Columbias border the Rockies, and their similarities are at least as important as their differences. For the purposes of this book it makes sense to bundle the ranges together, all the while acknowledging that the Columbias are indeed not the Rockies.

Set like jewels along this grand crown of the continent are the famous national parks: Rocky Mountain, Grand Teton, Yellowstone, Glacier, Waterton Lakes, Banff, and Jasper. Each one bursts with classic mountain scenery—high snowy peaks mirrored in clear, forest-rimmed alpine lakes, broad glaciers, deep valleys, powerful rivers, abundant wildlife.

But there are other places, less known yet equally grand: Colorado's Telluride Valley and the Great Sand Dunes National Monument; the Sangre de Cristo Range and the Rio Grande

gorge in New Mexico; Wyoming's Snowy and Wind River ranges; Montana's Mission Mountains and the splendid Bitterroots on the Idaho border. There are many more.

The names given to places in the Rockies are themselves the stuff of dreams for anyone who loves mountains. They are names of rivers, roads, peaks, valleys, and wilderness areas: River of No Return, Top of the World, Pass in the Clouds, Going-to-the-Sun, Deer Lodge, Beaverhead, Yoho, Assiniboine, Clearwater, Sweetwater, Monte Vista, Medicine Bow, Flaming Gorge, Seedskadee, Popo Agie, Absaroka, Beartooth, Valle Grande, and hundreds more just as musical sounding. If it seems that the people who put names to the Rocky Mountains must have wondered at them, and loved them, that's because they always have, and still do.

How long people have lived in the Rockies remains the subject of controversy. There is ample evidence that 20,000 years ago, humans were widespread in North America. However, they may have been here longer than that. Human bone fragments found in southern California are thought to be 48,000 years old.

The first Americans were probably nomadic hunters who walked across the Bering Strait from Asia. During the Ice Age, enormous glaciers locked up enough water to lower the oceans several hundred feet. All over the world, land appeared where there had been only water before. Between what is now Siberia and Alaska, there appeared a strip of dry land now called Beringia by scientists. It formed a sort of bridge between the continents— a very large bridge. If the sea were just 150 feet lower than at present, Beringia would have been 1,000 miles wide. It was exposed several times over the past 50,000 years and remained dry for as much as 10,000 years each time. It seems only natural that people and animals would have migrated that way.

At that time, North America was heavily populated with big exotic animals. Saber-toothed tigers, giant sloths, giant armadillos, camels, mastodons, yaks, giant beavers, horses, and more. Around 9,000 years ago, as the glaciers melted away, many of those animal species also disappeared. Why? Was it the climate, changing too fast for animals to adapt? Did human hunters kill too many of them? Or was it the combination of both factors?

Whatever the reason, as the big animals became extinct, some residents of the New World, particularly in Mexico and

Central America, turned to agriculture. They grew corn, squash, beans, and other crops and built stone cities whose ruins we wonder at today. Those people include the Inca, the Maya, the Aztec, and—in connection with the Rockies—the Anasazi, who built the famous, now-abandoned cliff dwellings at Colorado's Mesa Verde and other locations.

Over most of the Mountain West, however, the nomadic way of life adapted and survived. Mastodons disappeared, but there were plenty of other animals, notably bison, elk, deer, and sheep. With no domestic animals except dogs, and no metal tools, the people of the Rockies nonetheless developed a self-sustaining way of life.

When Europeans arrived in the Rocky Mountains, they found a fabulously rich land and they picked it like a plum.

The first were Spaniards, pushing north from Mexico in the early 1500s. Looking for gold, they skirted the southern fringe of the Rockies, became lost in the labyrinthine canyons of Utah, had trouble with Ute Indians, and gave up the search. They did, however, establish the province of New Mexico with its capital at Santa Fe. Almost 250 years later, in the middle 1700s, French and English fur traders made their way across the plains far enough to see snowy peaks in the distance. Although a few adventurers probably made it all the way to the Rockies in the 1700s (one, legend has it, was Daniel Boone), they left no record of their travels.

White settlement of the West really began in 1803 with the Louisiana Purchase, when the United States bought from Napoleon Bonaparte his claim to the entire Mississippi River drainage. The French had acquired it from Spain. The Spanish had claimed it merely by planting their flag at the mouth of the great river and declaring ownership of all the land it drained and of all its inhabitants. What the United States bought was not the land itself, but the French claim to it. The task remained of mapping it, conquering its human inhabitants, and populating it with Americans of European stock.

As a first step, President Thomas Jefferson sent Captains Meriwether Lewis and William Clark on their famous "journey of exploration." One of the expedition's primary goals was to investigate the feasibility of an inland water route up the Missouri River to the Pacific Ocean.

They found to their surprise that the continent was larger than they had thought. The Missouri did not lead to the Pacific Ocean; it provided only a route to the interior. The interior, however, was full of beaver. And that's where the fur trappers wanted to go.

There were never very many trappers working the mountains, yet it took them less than thirty years to trap out the beaver and put themselves out of business. Many of them turned then to buffalo hunting, scouting for the army, or guiding gold seekers and settlers bound for the West Coast. More than 60,000 migrants passed through Wyoming on the Oregon and California trails per summer. Of all those migrants, virtually none stopped to think that the Rockies might be worth investigating. The Mormon settlers were the exception; they came to build an independent farming society, and they came to stay. The others just hurried on through.

That changed with the discovery of gold in Colorado. The city of Denver burst into existence practically overnight. Miners flooded the high country, spilling over in all directions. Before long, they had found gold throughout the region, from New Mexico to British Columbia. Although most of the miners wanted only to make a fortune and go back home, others fell in love with the mountains and stayed.

Along with mining came other industries, giving birth to ranching, farming, shopkeeping, transport companies, railroads, local governments, and, inevitably, conflict with native inhabitants.

The two cultures—European and Indian—could not have been more dissimilar. Their differences had as much to do with religion and philosophy as with ownership of the land. The story of the resulting conflict, between settlers and those who would not be settled, is a sad chapter in the history of the continent.

Life in the Rocky Mountains has always been closely tied to the land itself, as the source of opportunity and as the chief limiting factor of growth. Perhaps nowhere else in this country do weather, topography, and geology have such an impact on the way people live—and on where they live. Western pioneers learned quickly that every valley was both a new opportunity and a new challenge and that their chances for success were closely related to their understanding of local geography. If a rancher picked the wrong side of a mountain or chose pastures that were just a little too high or too dry or too windy, he was doomed to failure. If a railway surveyor ignored the way winter snows drifted along his proposed route or how many avalanche paths crossed the tracks, he guaranteed that the railway would not survive.

Today, the people who live in the Rocky Mountain region still walk a narrow line between opportunity and natural, land-based constraints. Their history has largely been one of exploitation, living by what they call a resource-based economy. That means finding something to sell—furs, meat, minerals, oil, timber, hydroelectric power, recreation, unspoiled scenery. These items, however, are primary resources, products of the land. They are either nonrenewable or limited in supply. When they run out or run low, populations and economies fade away or stop growing, until an alternative is found. The pattern has repeated itself uncounted times throughout the West. The search for long-term options remains one of the most important challenges facing Rocky Mountain economies today.

Of all the reasons people have for choosing to live in the Rockies, perhaps the most easily understood is their beauty. The Rockies never look better than in the fall—a short but perfect season. It starts at the end of August when meadows turn brown and flowers go to seed. A cold sharpness appears in the night air; after hot days under a strong sun, you want a jacket. In early September, there is often a stormy spell—rain or sleet falls in the valleys and you see snow on the mountains when the clouds break. But winter is still two months or more away. That high snow vanishes and Indian summer dominates much of September and October. Days are pleasant and dry, while nights freeze hard enough that ice covers shallow ponds and the banks of rivers are white with hoarfrost.

Fall engenders bittersweet feelings among residents of the Rockies. You know that the snow, once it comes, will linger into May or June. As much as you might love the winter, even look forward to it, you also know that by April your affection for snow and ice will be worn mighty thin. So as you watch September become October, a part of you is already nostalgic for summer.

Even so, I welcome autumn as the most spectacular time of the year. Everything is moving and changing. Fall colors light up the hills. In Colorado, whole mountainsides, covered with as-

pen, turn brilliant gold; in Canada, alpine larch are just as bright. They are joined throughout the range by willows, cottonwoods, mountain ash, and a variety of shrubs. Even high above timberline, where there are no trees, dwarf shrubs ignite in the same brilliant colors.

Migratory birds gather in flocks for their journey south: blackbirds, cedar waxwings, Arctic pipits, sandhill cranes, and Canada geese. Large animals migrate too, not down south but downhill, from the high country to sheltered winter range. They look handsome and healthy in new winter coats. For many of them, fall is mating season. Elk are bugling, bison are tearing up the meadows, bighorn rams are smashing heads, and bull moose are going around destroying small trees with their antlers.

You can't miss hearing the elk when they bugle. There is no other sound—not a bird song, not the whine of mosquitoes, not wind in the pines, not the yammering howl of coyotes—that is as full of the season's importance as a bull elk's bugle. Almost anywhere in the Rockies during October you can hear it: half-scream, half-bellow, pure hormonal urgency. It echoes through silent, damp woodland in the gray dusk, mysterious and powerful. It rings across moonlit meadows in the middle of the night, and if you are sleeping in the open, you can hear the thud of hooves on frozen ground. They are the hooves of excited elk cows and prancing bulls.

Then, with a single heavy storm, winter arrives. The trees have long since lost their leaves. The seeds of flowering plants have fallen to earth. The ground itself is frozen and ready. By late November, the snow is often 1 to 3 feet deep. You won't see the ground again until April or even May.

No question about it, mountain winters are hard, but they are also beautiful. Storms rarely last long. They move through with great force, leaving behind clear, sunny days and a sparkling landscape. The long subzero cold spells that plague the Midwest are virtually unknown in the Intermountain West. Nights get terribly cold, because the air is thin and dry and the atmosphere does not hold the heat (the record, set at Rogers Pass in Montana, is −69.9°F). But thin air also means that the alpine sun has great strength. It's not at all unusual to see temperature fluctuations of 50 degrees or more in the space of six hours, from minus 30 just before dawn to plus 20 at noon.

For people living in the Rockies, it means that winter is a time not for hibernation, but for active outdoor pursuits. If you don't ski or do something else outside, you might as well migrate with the birds. Or wish you had.

Every so often, we get a winter of really intense cold and then the problems show up. Pipes freeze, vehicles refuse to run, heating bills soar, wood supplies run low, and life in general becomes oppressive. I lived at Old Faithful in Yellowstone Park during my first Rocky Mountain winters, in a house provided by my employer. It was warm and well built. Nothing ever went wrong with it. Nor did I have to deal with an auto. I skied wherever I went and I never felt the need to go far. Lacking any concern for my own comfort or the cost of maintaining it, I reveled in temperature extremes. I loved the big storms. One March, 10 feet fell in a week. Small buildings disappeared, and I thought it was absolutely wonderful. I worried only for the elk and bison that stoically endured, day after day, the most arduous conditions imaginable. They impressed me with what I took to be their tremendous spirit, their unending natural dignity.

After some years, I left the park and lived once again where cars had to be started, roads plowed, pipes kept from freezing, utility bills paid, and I felt for the first time the weight and frustration of a long, hard winter. I came to have great respect for my neighbors—for the mechanics, the builders, the ranchers, the teachers, the parents. That was a hard winter. By March, the pressure was showing. Smiles had grown thin. Shaky marriages had shaken apart. Some people had packed up and left until spring. Or they just plain moved to Arizona and never came back.

Of course, winter always ends, always reluctantly, dragging its heels, sometimes shouting abuse in the form of snowstorms in May and June—and even, some years, in July. It gives way first in the valley bottoms, then on south-facing slopes, then gradually up the mountains. Snow endures in deep forest well into June and on the high peaks well into July. The season changes so gradually that some people say there is no spring in the mountains: "Eleven months of winter, two weeks of summer and two weeks of fall." So the saying goes.

But if you look, the signs are there. You can smell the warming earth. You watch the days grow longer. The birds come back. Robins and sandhill cranes head north before the snow has melted from valley floors. Ruby-crowned kinglets are also early arrivals, tiny birds with an audacious call: Dewy, dewy, dewy, dewy, dweep! Black-throated hummingbirds push the season too, arriving mysteriously before flowers bloom. Trumpeter swans and bald eagles, having wintered along open waterways, disperse to nesting areas. Curlews probe the mud of marshes with their long bills, while from overhead on quiet evenings, you hear snipe making their odd whiffling sound. For me, however, the big event is the day I hear the first hermit thrush calling from deep in the forest. Then I think about planting flowers in the garden.

Well before that happens, the big animals have made changes of their own. In April, elk are dropping their antlers and returning to summer ranges. Bison cows drop calves of a startling red color. Coyotes, so vocal a month earlier, are silent now, gone secretively to dens. And if you pay attention to tracks in the snow and mud, there's a good chance of finding evidence that bears have waked from their winter sleep.

Among the plants, willows are putting out furry buds. Aspen trees display tiny blossoms. Along the line of receding snowbanks, early flowers bloom: spring beauties, glacier lilies, pasqueflowers, and others.

Somewhere along the line, you realize that summer has come and with it a great impatience. Summer is a time of wild abandon, of willy-nilly growth and botanic tumult. Time is limited and everything is timed to take full advantage of the season. Elk calves, born in April, are ready to begin eating grass just as the grass is ready to be eaten. Animals feed earnestly. Insects appear with the snap of the season's fingers. It's amazing how fast things can turn green. Whole meadows go bright with wildflowers overnight. Their fragrance fills the air. Caught up in the spirit of the season, people try to grow tomatoes outdoors, even though they know better. Summer is too short, and so beautiful that it can hurt.

Yet summer can also be punishing. Once the snow has melted, rain is needed. If the rains fail, as they did in 1979 and again in 1988, drought conditions result. Plants dry up earlier than normal. In July, forests and meadows look like they should in August. Fires, when they start, can be devastating.

But not even fires will stop elk from bugling, or willows from turning red, or ice from forming on the lip of an alpine pond. Summer gives way to autumn, and the circle of the year is renewed.

17

An old cabin speaks of the hardships faced by early settlers. It wasn't so much the severity of winters as their length that made life difficult for pioneers.

Willard Clay

20

Pat O'Hara

A cold moon sets behind icy, dawn-tinted peaks in the Canadian Rockies. Purple is a color often associated with dawn and dusk during the coldest weather. Although lower in elevation, the massive grandeur of the northern Rockies is enhanced by horizontal lines of sedimentary strata.

Pat O'Hara

The last light of day touches the summit of Mount Burgess in Yoho National Park, British Columbia, Canada. *Yoho* is a Cree Indian word meaning "wonderful."

Sunrise at Great Sand Dunes National Monument, Colorado.

Part One
Summit Country

Sunset on the Elk Mountains, White River National Forest, Colorado.

THE SOUTHERN ROCKIES

In 1858 Julia Holmes wrote home to the East Coast about her climb of Pikes Peak, an experience that she said "fills the mind with infinitude, and sends the soul to God."

Julia was twenty years old. She had come from Kansas with her husband James and a small party of prospectors to look for gold. They had no luck at mining, but they enjoyed the mountains immensely. In August, she and James packed light loads and set off for the summit of Pikes Peak. They weren't explorers, they were holidaymakers. The trip was a lark, a pleasant summer outing. "Think," wrote Julia, "of the huge rocks projecting out in all imaginable shapes, with the beautiful evergreens, the pines, the firs, the spruces, interspersed among them and the clear cold mountain stream . . . rushing, tumbling, hissing down over the rough mountain sides."

The Holmeses had the good fortune of seeing Colorado's Front Range just before the Pikes Peak gold rush. One year later the place was crowded with miners who had no interest in beautiful evergreens and little desire to climb mountains just for the view. But they sure knew about Pikes Peak. Somehow that mountain, neither the highest nor the most impressive in the Front Range, came to represent the whole strange world of the southern Rockies. Settlers and prospectors took up the motto "Pikes Peak or Bust" even though their destination, the new boomtown—Denver—was 50 miles north of Pikes Peak.

As they soon realized, the Colorado Rockies were much more than a single range of mountains. Pioneers found a broad series of subranges packed one upon the other, a vast complexity of terrain. The Front Range was the first seen. Behind it lay ranges they would come to know as Gore, Park, Never Summer, Tarryall, Mosquito, Mummy, Elk, San Juan, Sawatch, La Garita, Uinta, and more—all of them in the Rockies, but each range distinct from the others.

The territory went on, apparently, forever. The Rockies dwarfed New England. They were bigger than Europe. No one knew back then the true extent of the Mountain West. They had no idea that the summits near Pikes Peak were only the southern end of a range that stretched nearly 2,000 miles northward.

Not just mountains, but a stunning variety of landforms awaited discovery. There were deep canyons, high plateaus, miniature deserts beneath snowy peaks, shadowed forests, rock-rimmed lakes, and windswept but fertile basins. And beyond the Rockies was the strangest country that eastern-born folks could ever imagine. People who had seen the Appalachians or the Adirondacks could understand mountains and snow and wild animals, but what could they make of that shimmering land of red rocks stretching like a scene from the Bible across Utah? What of the Southwest desert with its bizarre cacti and scaly lizards? Or the great desert canyons occupied by bad-tempered rivers? In the

East, except during spring runoff, rivers flowed gently. They provided natural routes of travel. Before highways and railroads were built, rivers were the lifeblood of commerce. But out here in the West, rivers behaved like wild animals, tumbling through the mountains between grim rock walls. Few alpine rivers were navigable. Like a lot of other things in the West, you learned to keep your distance and your footing.

The whole darn place was ornery. Pioneers from the East learned to cope with a new set of dangers in the mountains: not just wild rivers but avalanches, landslides, flash floods, grizzlies, rattlesnakes, vast waterless expanses where you could die of thirst in a couple of days, and snowstorms so sudden that wagons would be buried overnight and pioneer parties would wake up to the brutal white face of death by starvation. In 1856, 202 Mormon immigrants headed for a new home in Utah were trapped and killed by an early winter storm at South Pass, Wyoming.

The Rockies may have seemed a cruel landscape at first experience. But the more people learned about the Mountain West and how to cope with its challenges, the more they came to love it. Their understanding gave birth to a fierce loyalty. The winters weren't so terrible after all; January in Colorado was a whole lot warmer than in Minnesota. Spring came early to the lower valleys. Summer was just flat-out gorgeous. The dry, clear air eventually grew on a person until he or she never wanted to see a humid climate again. There was plenty of water to drink, after all, and so what if you couldn't raise corn in the mountains? You could run cattle instead.

Even the terrain was less forbidding than it first appeared. Every turn brought something new and fabulous. Just as the mountains got higher and the canyons got deeper, a huge open valley with shoulder-high grass would appear with a gentle stream running through it that was shaded by groves of cottonwood. Here was paradise; the whole West was paradise. If you liked this sort of country, you couldn't live anywhere else. Anything you needed could be found here; if you didn't find it you could always dream. The Rockies attracted plenty of dreamers. They still do.

❧

We can only speculate on the hopes and ambitions of the first people, but it seems likely that their thoughts were on animals. They arrived in the southern Rockies about 15,000 years ago, when the hunting was good for a huge variety of wildlife, including mammoths, giant bison, and others that are now extinct. Only in recent times, as such animals disappeared, did some people turn to agriculture for a significant portion of their food. The Anasazi, for example, were living in simple villages and growing crops about 1,500 years ago. They built their famous cliff dwellings, like the ones at Mesa Verde, during the twelfth century. The Anasazi, however, were not mountain people. They lived on the fringes of the Rockies, as do their modern descendants, the Pueblo people of the Rio Grande Valley in New Mexico.

We know more about the next wave of dreamers: Spanish soldiers under Coronado, pursuing visions of gold and the fabled Seven Cities of Cíbola. The year was 1540, almost a century before the Pilgrims landed at Plymouth Rock. Instead of golden cities, Coronado found the adobe villages of Pueblo Indians. Disappointed, Coronado performed some halfhearted pillaging and retreated southward. Later, in 1596, the Spanish returned to establish a colony that lasted some 250 years with only one interruption. That happened in 1680 when the Pueblos, under a medicine man with the unlikely name of Popé, organized a successful and bloody revolt, driving the Europeans from New Mexico. They returned, of course, twelve years later with a heavily weighted fist.

Throughout that time, lines of communication and support between Spanish Mexico and New Mexico were never very strong. Santa Fe was hundreds of difficult miles from Mexico City, through country controlled by Apache Indians. Supply trains risked the journey only once every three years and sometimes failed to make it at all. Living in such isolation, Spanish settlers were forced by the hard facts of the landscape to develop an indigenous way of life. Much of this they learned from the Indians, whose society they had meant to enlighten. The two groups were forced to borrow from each other, developing, if not friendship, a wary coexistence.

Then came the Mexican-American War of 1847. The American army invaded New Mexico with a whole new set of cultural values, demanding new allegiance to yet another distant government. This time Indian and Spaniard resisted together and suffered the bloody results side by side. American law was enforced but never embraced; peace came as a result of reluctant, some-

26

times minimal accommodation. Today, the Rio Grande Valley is celebrated as much for its three distinct cultures as for a mountain landscape that has inspired generations of artists and writers. Looking at the country around Santa Fe, you get the feeling that the real conquerors, from the time before even the Pueblo Indians, are the mountains. Everyone eventually succumbs to them, adjusts to them, and learns to love them.

There are actually two mountain ranges at Santa Fe, flanking the Rio Grande Valley: the Sangre de Cristo Range on the east topped by Wheeler Peak, the highest point in New Mexico; and the Jemez Mountains on the west. Both were caused by block faulting. The earth's surface, broken into huge blocks of stone, moved along fault lines. The blocks that are now mountains moved up and apart while the block between them (now the Rio Grande Valley) remained relatively stationary. The result is a rift valley extending from southern New Mexico to central Colorado, similar to the more famous one in East Africa and also the scene of geologic instability and volcanism.

The fusion of desert and mountain gives northern New Mexico its distinct character, marked by big sweeping views, big thunderstorms, big sunsets, and clear air that you find only in deserts. The mountains have space around them. You top a rise high in the Sangre de Cristos and you see spread before you not another mountain valley, but a magnificent expanse of desert stretching off a hundred miles or more. In the summer, tremendous thunderstorms cruise on anvil sails. They drop curtains of rain that might never reach the ground, but you can smell it. You smell the water mixing with dust churned up by the winds under those storms. Combined with the scent of juniper trees and the electricity in the air, it is an unforgettable perfume, the fragrant signature of the southern Rockies.

From Santa Fe, the Sangre de Cristos run arrow straight into Colorado. The Jemez Mountains, although less spectacular in appearance, claim the distinction of carrying the Continental Divide, which seems intent on making a rambling tour of the entire region. It rolls leisurely northward along the high cattle range of the Jemez, enters Colorado without fanfare, and suddenly takes a left-hand turn on an ambitious sortie among the rugged San Juan Mountains. Gone are the spacious skies and desert views of New Mexico. Gone are the sweeping grasslands

and lingering sunsets. Suddenly the peaks are precipitous crags squeezed together above somber canyons where not even water seems to lie flat. The San Juans are mining country, sliced by jeep roads, perforated by tunnels, dotted with decayed prospectors' shacks. With numerous peaks over 14,000 feet high and not a single tillable acre, San Juan County is a good place if you like rock and a horror if you like farms.

Nor, in contrast to the pueblos of New Mexico, is it good for history. The oldest San Juan settlements were founded not much more than a century ago. Many of those died in their youth when the minerals ran out. Today, even their names are forgotten. The country carries much older Spanish titles. Rivers include El Rio de las Animas Perdidas, Los Pinos, Florida, La Plata, Saguache, Cochetopa, Piedra, Dolores, and San Miguel. Their waters melt off mountains named Conejos, Del Norte, La Garita, and San Luis. Salted among them are a few surviving non-Spanish names like Sawpit, Ironton, Powderhorn, and the lovely Slumgullion Pass.

From near the town of Silverton, the Divide heads back east across the La Garita Mountains to the range called Sawatch, the anglicized spelling of the Spanish version, *Saguache*, of a Ute Indian name meaning "blue earth spring." More layered nomenclature. Compared to the vertiginous San Juans, the broad-shouldered Sawatch might seem rather gentle were it not for their elevation. Taken together, they comprise the highest group of mountains in Colorado and therefore the highest in the Rockies: Mount Elbert (14,433 feet), La Plata Peak (14,336 feet), Mount Antero (14,269 feet).

For some odd geologic reason, the Divide runs north past this line of peaks without actually touching their summits. It cuts close to the former mining town (now ski mecca) of Aspen before again jogging eastward toward Denver past more famous mining towns: Leadville, Fairplay, and Breckenridge. Everything is high here, even the towns. Fairplay is 9,953 feet high. Leadville robs you of breath at 10,152 feet. Until the Eisenhower Memorial Tunnel was completed under the Divide in 1973, all vehicles coming this way, including traffic on Interstate 70, were forced to cross 11,992-foot Loveland Pass. It's no wonder they named this place Summit County.

We are now in the Front Range, overlooking Denver. The

27

Divide at this point is about 70 miles from Pikes Peak and as far east as it can go. It turns north, following the Indian Peaks into Rocky Mountain National Park all the way to the park's north boundary, and then like a wandering tourist it turns back to the south, then west, then north and northwest along the ridge of the Park Range to Wyoming.

For the record, Colorado boasts some fifteen separate mountain ranges; the headwaters of major rivers including the Colorado, Platte, Arkansas, Rio Grande, and San Juan; the biggest human population in the Rockies (although some would argue that Denver and Colorado Springs are on the edge of the Rockies, not in them); and the highest peaks in the Rockies. As a raw statistic, the last of these claims is indisputable. Colorado owns all forty-four Rocky Mountain summits over 14,000 feet. There isn't another one anywhere in the range. But raw statistics rarely quell controversy, and partisans of the Canadian Rockies are quick to defend their less lofty peaks, the highest of which is Mount Robson, a mere 12,972 feet. You could stand New York's World Trade Center on its summit and still the proponents of Colorado supremacy would look down from above. Never mind that, say the backers of Mount Robson, when it comes to measuring mountains, the absolute height is not important. What matters is the distance from base to summit, the relief. How high do the mountains stick up out of the ground? What do they look like?

The point is well taken. Altitude—at least in terms of visual impact—can be a relative phenomenon. Pikes Peak is well below the average elevation of Tibet, where mere hills rise over 20,000 feet.

Mount Robson, with its humble 12,972-foot summit, nevertheless has a 7,800-foot north face dripping with glaciers, battered by violent storms, and alive with avalanches. Robson is one of the world's most dangerous mountains. Its weather is horrendous. There is no easy way to climb it, even for world-class alpinists. In terms of climate, the summit of Robson is perhaps a mile higher than anything in Colorado. One thing is certain. Unlike Pikes Peak, no entrepreneur will ever put a vehicle road up Robson. No flowers grow on its summit. And there are definitely no foot races to the top.

The reason has as much to do with latitude as altitude. Going up in elevation is similar to traveling north toward the Arctic, where summers are short, trees cannot grow, and the ground is permanently frozen. A high mountain in the southern Rockies can have a climate similar to that of a low mountain in the north.

This is true of all the world's mountains. In Africa, Mount Kilimanjaro, located almost on the equator, holds its ice-capped head in the Arctic. In the case of the Rockies, it is interesting to notice how they rise as they come south: In effect, their increasing altitude compensates for the effects of decreasing latitude. For example, timberline in Glacier National Park (Montana) is around 6,500 feet, beneath peaks of about 10,000 feet. Timberline in Colorado near Aspen is much higher, around 11,500 feet, beneath peaks of about 14,000 feet. In both places, snow-covered mountains rise several thousand feet above forested slopes, making them *seem* about the same height. Did someone plan it this way?

Things have changed a lot since Julia Holmes so eagerly climbed Pikes Peak (after living for a time in New Mexico, she returned to the East Coast). The Ute Indians are all but gone from their old territory. The gold and silver towns of Central City, Fairplay, Breckenridge, Creede, Cripple Creek, and Aspen among others, having burst into existence, still survive. Ranches spread across the state. The trails of Indians and prospectors and fur trappers were replaced by railroads and highways. Santa Fe and Aspen became favored destinations among the jet set and the stars of motion pictures, a possibility that Julia, for all her wide-eyed anticipation of the future, could never have imagined.

If she could see it today, she might laugh at the commercial bustle near Pikes Peak—the cog railway, the alpine slide, the "World's Only Completely Lighted Canyon and Waterfall," and best of all from her perspective, the Pikes Peak Ghost Town. She would certainly write home about the toll road that winds to the summit. But if she went there on a summer evening when the air was clear and stood looking out to the west at the Rockies, fading row upon row into the sunset, she would know where she was and she would think the view was very fine indeed.

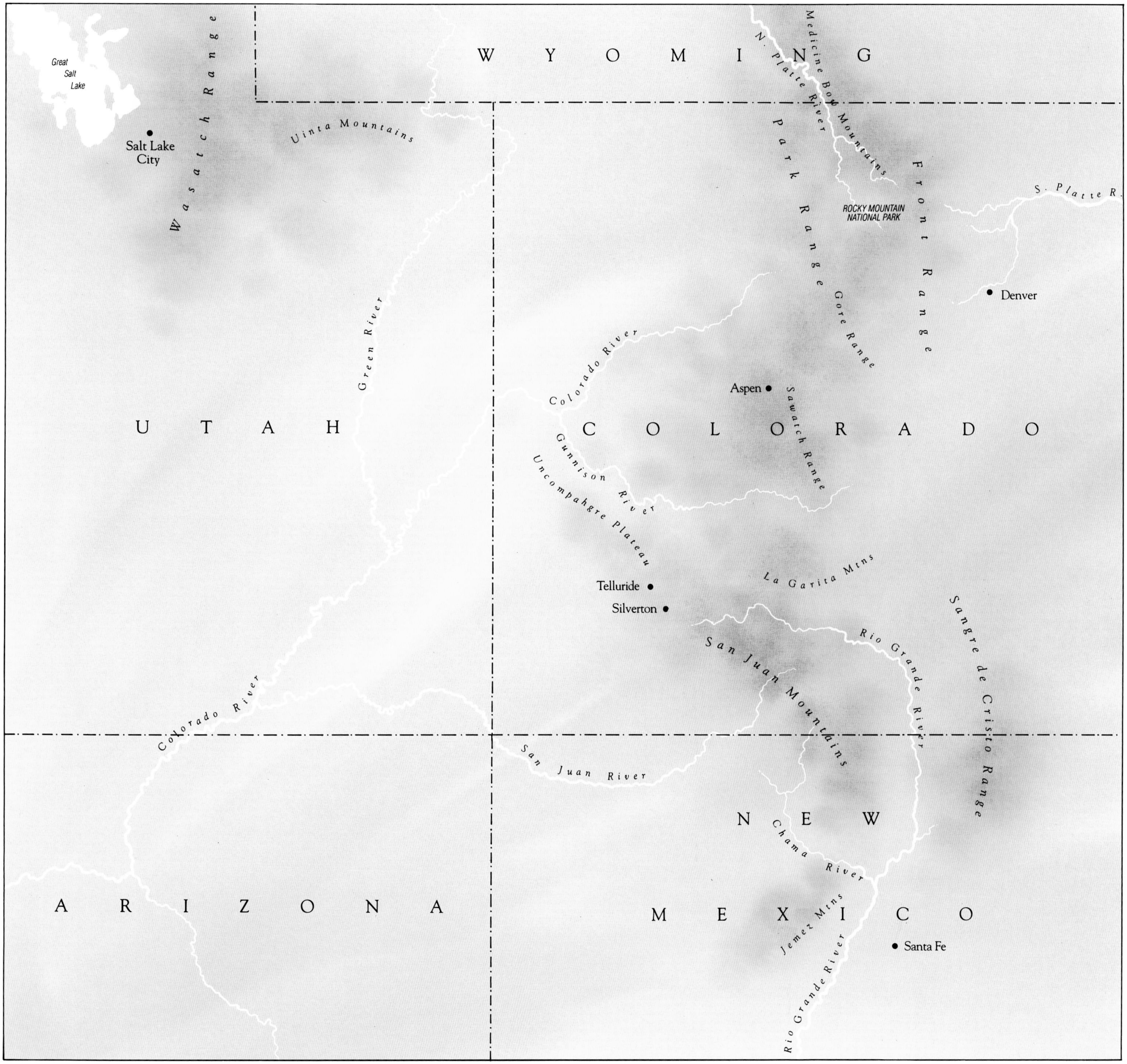

Great
Salt
Lake

W Y O M I N G

Medicine Bow Mountains

N. Platte River

Park Range

Wasatch Range

Salt Lake
City

Uinta Mountains

ROCKY MOUNTAIN
NATIONAL PARK

Front Range

Gore Range

S. Platte R.

Denver

Green River

Colorado River

Aspen

Sawatch Range

U T A H

C O L O R A D O

Gunnison River

Uncompahgre Plateau

Telluride

Silverton

La Garita Mtns

Sangre de Cristo Range

Rio Grande River

San Juan Mountains

Colorado River

San Juan River

N E W

Chama River

A R I Z O N A

M E X I C O

Jemez Mtns

Santa Fe

Rio Grande River

Willard Clay

The Rockies promise much and demand much. For a farmer, the difference between success and failure can be a matter of a few miles. One end of a valley might receive abundant rain at the right time of year, allowing crops and pastures to flourish, but just over the ridge, desert conditions prevail. Especially in the drier stretches of the southern Rockies, you can watch clouds drop moisture on nearby mountains as you sift the powdery dust of an abandoned farm through your fingers.

These two Spanish mission churches, at Chimayo (*left*) and Trampas, are built of adobe, a material well suited to the dry New Mexico Rockies. Made of native earth mixed with straw, adobe lends buildings the appearance of having grown up from the soil—a truly indigenous architecture.

32

Pat O'Hara

Telluride, Colorado, named for its native ore (a combination of gold, silver, and tellurium), was a booming town a hundred years ago during the heyday of silver mining in the San Juan Mountains. In the 1960s, with the mines closed, the town came close to dying. Commercial lots on Main Street sold for back taxes; houses went for the value of a used car. That's all changed today; skiing and mountain tourism have given Telluride a new life.

Kathy Clay

Kathy Clay

The indomitable spirit of small mountain towns is reflected by spirited celebrations like this Fourth of July parade in Silverton, Colorado, just over the Divide from Telluride. Silverton's miners have mostly gone elsewhere, but the Rockies continue to attract new people with dreams and the energy to make them come true.

Larry Ulrich

W. Perry Conway

Higher slopes in the Rockies, like this meadow at Dallas Pass in the San Juan Mountains, are too cold and their soil is too thin to grow crops. Instead, they support aspen and conifer forests, scrubby stands of gambel oak, a great variety of summer wildflowers, and grazing animals—not only domestic cattle requiring fences, but elk and (*above*) mule deer as well.

36

Willard Clay

Building a wooden fence may seem a laborious task compared to running a few strands of barbed wire but anyone who's tried to dig postholes in rocky, nearly impenetrable soil will tell you that it's a whole lot easier to stack aspen poles in a free-standing, self-supporting zigzag. Here, sneezeweed blossoms beside a fence in the San Juan Mountains.

Pat O'Hara

The San Miguel Mountains of southwest Colorado provide a stunning backdrop for a hard way of life. High pastures are good for summer grazing only. To make a living and to support cattle through the winter, a rancher needs irrigated bottomland for growing hay and alfalfa.

Summer thunderheads over Longs Peak in Rocky Mountain National Park, Colorado.

GHOSTS OF GOLD

It could be said that the Colorado gold rush began with a sack of dirt. A wagoner named John Cantrell, having hauled a load of freight to Utah, was on his way home past the eastern foothills of the Rockies. Upon reaching the South Platte River, he met a party of prospectors who had found a small amount of gold in the riverbank. Cantrell scooped up some of the earth in question and carried it east in a sack.

In Kansas City, Cantrell gathered a crowd and put on a gold panning demonstration. Eureka! Gold in that dirt! Not much, but enough. Gold in the Rockies, fellas! Gold for the taking.

The story spread, reinforcing other rumors. Perhaps 100,000 prospectors set out in the autumn and winter of 1858 and 1859, a horde of excited people heading west toward a tent city that would later become Denver. Many of those who started the journey, discouraged by distance and uncertainty, turned back partway. Tens of thousands, however, made it to the Rockies—in wagons, on horseback, or on foot, armed with gold pans, shovels, and expectations of laying quick claim to rich ground.

The problem was there was no gold in Denver. Cantrell's sack of dirt was about all anyone had found beneath the foothills. No one knew where to look next. Winter had closed the high country and Denver swelled with restless men.

Not everyone was in Denver, however. George Jackson, a man with wide experience in the West, lived in a cabin a few miles north. He was hunting elk one day on the South Fork of Clear Creek, when he stooped to check the frozen creekbed gravel. Eureka! Word got back to Denver and the rush was on.

Jackson's discovery was only the beginning. He had found the key that eventually opened the door to the entire Rockies. As one creekbed filled with miners, the overflow spilled west, over the ridges, deeper into the mountains, west to Utah, south to Spanish country, north into what we now call Montana and Idaho. In less than two decades, the mountains were overrun. Miners probed every crevice, every ravine, chasing their dreams of fortune with almost fanatic energy. Meanwhile, another rush got started in Canada's Fraser River Valley, drawing more prospectors from the West Coast.

It was a frantic time for the players in this game of instant wealth. They all knew the gold would run out before long and that only a few would actually strike it rich. They all heard the fabulous and sometimes true stories of claims yielding gold by the pound and even the ton. Tons! Scoop it up with a shovel! No wonder they stampeded from rumor to rumor, from one mining camp to another, dancing to the wild tune of Fortune's fiddle.

You can trace their paths through Colorado on a modern highway map. Beginning in Denver, the hopeful tide spread to Central City, Breckenridge, Fairplay, Aspen, Silverton, Telluride, and many points in-between, moving along a broad band extending from mid-Colorado toward the Southwest. Their locations practically define what geologists call the Colorado Mineral Belt.

We need to go back about 100 million years to understand why gold is found in some places and not others. Back then, the inner part of the continent, including what is now the Rocky Mountain region, was a shallow sea covering layers of sediment as much as 2.5 miles thick. The sediments had eroded off ancient mountains farther west than the modern Rockies and also off two great ranges, called the ancestral Rockies, that came into being around 300 million years ago and then eroded down to nothing.

The sediments settled in neat, undisturbed layers and eventually hardened into rock.

Then, about 70 million years ago, the uplift that gave birth to the Rocky Mountains began its movements. The continent had been quiet for a long time but now it was shifting again, rising and stretching. The shallow sea drained away, its swampy coastline moving slowly east as the old seafloor rose. The higher the land rose, the more it was affected by erosion. Water, wind, and gravity carved separate mountains, plateaus, and river valleys.

That, essentially, describes what we see today in the Canadian Rockies—big mountains of sedimentary rock. They have been twisted, tilted, and folded, but the old sedimentary layers are essentially intact.

Things are different in Colorado. Gold miners don't care much about sedimentary rocks. Limestone, sandstone, shale, and conglomerate are virtually sterile of precious metals. What matters to a miner is what lies beneath. He looks for the old, crystalline rock of the continental foundation, formed from the molten mineral stew of the earth's beginnings.

This ancient rock—granite, gneiss, and schist—has been cracked by earth movements and altered by pressure and heat. Over the ages, molten material rich in minerals forced its way under pressure into the cracks. While this material cooled, gold and other metals condensed to form the mineral veins sought so eagerly by miners. As a point of interest, the goldfields of British Columbia were discovered immediately to the west of the Canadian Rockies in mountains 100 million years or so older than the Rockies and composed not of sediments but of old hard rocks.

But let's return to Colorado, to the time when sediments rose and erosion cut them apart. Some 20 million years after the first big uplift, things began to happen again. Volcanoes erupted, not once but many times. Repeated lava flows built entire new ranges—the Flat Tops, the West Elks, the San Juans. Some volcanoes spewed ash and lava, only to collapse and then erupt again. This went on for millions of years, making a mess of the old neat sedimentary mountains.

As if that was not enough, 28 million years ago the Rockies in general rose an additional 5,000 feet. This second uplift rejuvenated the erosion process. Even more sedimentary rock was carried away, finally revealing the ancient crystalline rocks; in effect, the continental basement had been heaved up into the weather. There was treasure buried in that basement.

Where the old rock came to the surface, and where it had been broken apart enough to contain mineral veins, miners found precious metals. If only your great-grandfather could have seen that map in 1855 . . .

There are two kinds of gold mining—placer (pronounced "plasser") and hard rock. Placer gold is loose gold, flakes and nuggets cut out of the veins by erosion. Heavier than rock, the gold settles to the bottom of streambeds, sinking into the gravel and sand.

Almost all the early discoveries in Colorado were placer mines. It was an easy business to get started in: All you really needed, besides a claim, was a shovel and a pan. You could dig up the gravel, swirl it with water in the pan, let the stones wash out, and you'd be left with gold. George Jackson, when he made his find, had only an iron cup, a knife, and a hatchet. But that was enough.

Placer claims never lasted long. After the gravel and soil were sifted down to bedrock and the bedrock itself scoured clean, three things remained: a ruined valley, a group of newly rich men, and a big, big question. Where did the gold come from in the first place? Where is the vein, the mother lode? Sometimes the miners never found it. The veins had long ago eroded away, leaving only the placer gold. But in many cases, veins were discovered, and that was the beginning of a whole different story, hard-rock mining.

Had it not been for hard-rock mining, we might not have

such places as Aspen, Silverton, and Breckenridge in Colorado; Park City, Utah; Butte, Montana; Kellogg, Idaho; Kimberley, British Columbia; and others. Hard-rock mining, or deep mining, required big capital. Tunnels and shafts had to be dug and maintained. The process involved expensive tools, water pumps, drills, hoists, miles of cable, underground railroads, power plants, and organized crews of miners.

Through careful management, a good deep mine could produce for years at a sustainable, sometimes predictable rate. That attracted rich eastern investors. Westerners don't like to admit the fact, but it was, and continues to be, outside investment that sustains their way of life.

Deep mines changed the pattern of western settlement. They transformed mining camps filled with transient fortune seekers into mining towns whose residents expected to stay for a while. Although an ordinary but energetic man could acquire and develop a placer claim, get rich in the process, and then leave, he could not afford to operate a deep mine of any size. The best he could hope for was to discover a good vein, stake his claim, and sell out to a large, well-financed company.

Very few managed to do even that. But perhaps better for the majority, deep mines provided a man with a job and a steady wage. He could build a house, court a wife, have a family, and see his kids go to school. He could make plans.

If he didn't care to be a miner, he had plenty of choices. He could teach at the school. He could open a general store, or start a farm or a ranch to supply townspeople with meat. He could set up a sawmill. He could be a carpenter. He could hire out with horses and a wagon to carry loads or help build the railroads that soon reached the remotest mountain communities. He could even enter politics. A thousand enterprises flourished as a result of hard-rock mining; they could survive as long as the mines did and maybe longer.

Not that the deep mines were any kind of employment mecca. Wages were low and working conditions were terrible. Labor reform was far in the future. Dying in the mines was considered merely a risk of the job. People died outside the mines too, from an array of hazards including fires, explosions, avalanches, toxic smelter fumes, and, eventually, inevitably, labor strife. The battles between miners' unions and mine owners were nothing less than small wars complete with sabotage, bombings, riots, and scores of casualties. The miners almost always lost.

It's something to keep in mind when admiring the quaint artifacts of the mining boom.

Eventually, of course, even the great mines gave out. Or they went too deep and mine tunnels filled with water. Or the market price fell. One of the worst events for Colorado silver mines (Silverton, Creede, and Aspen among others) was the repeal of the Sherman Silver Purchase Act in 1893. Only in effect for three years, the act had required the federal government to purchase large quantities of silver, far more than needed for coinage. It was meant to support the price of silver at a time when worldwide supplies were fast increasing. It may have slowed the price decline somewhat, but the value of silver continued to fall as the economy inflated. Mines were struggling before the Purchase Act was repealed; afterward, many closed for good. One after another, fabulously rich mining districts suffered the same fate: boom then bust, from richer to poorer. Wherever it was, from the San Juan Mountains to the Front Range, from Telluride to Aspen to the mines of Idaho and British Columbia, the gold—or silver, or copper, or whatever—played out, and then what?

Hard times, for most mining towns. Almost totally dependent on a single industry, their fortunes fell with the mines. Some towns died entirely. Others limped along with reduced populations and lowered expectations. But if there's one thing people in the Rockies have always been good at, it's being resourceful—finding some way to make a living in the place they have chosen as home, whatever that takes.

The days of easy fortune are gone, but mining continues in a less dramatic style for coal, lead, zinc, molybdenum, bentonite, uranium, trona, oil, and even some gold. Some towns, more diversified to begin with, thrive as ranching, farming, timber, and transportation centers. Recreation, in all its widely increasing forms, is a major growth industry, particularly skiing in former mining towns such as Aspen, Telluride, Breckenridge, and Park City.

Some towns discovered the value of their rusting relics. Silverton is a case in point. At the difficult elevation of 9,318 feet, Silverton occupies one of the rare flat spots in the San Juan Range. Not many people live there. Ramshackle buildings stand empty. Nights are as quiet as the inside of a mine shaft.

A century ago it was a boomtown, the seat of a county that took up most of southwest Colorado and boasted a population of 5,000. Quite a few people were getting rich fast, and those who hadn't figured it was only a matter of time. They had good reason for hope. Before it was over, some $300 million worth of precious metal had been dug out of the San Juans and carted off to smelters.

Silverton hit its peak after 1890. Then the boom ended. Mines closed. The economy shriveled and the miners moved away. Most of Silverton's history since then has been a story of stubborn but steady decline. San Juan County, once so big, was reduced in size. Today it contains thousands of abandoned mine sites, hundreds of miles of underground tunnels, not one acre of farmland, and only a few hundred people.

Of those, many are summer residents. They leave when the snow flies. Others enjoy peaceful winters. They point out that there are some economic benefits of decline: The same little Victorian house that would sell for $100,000 or more in Aspen is advertised at "$40,000 or best offer" (including not one but three city lots) in Silverton.

Besides that, Silverton, although diminished from its heyday, is far from a ghost town. At about noon every day from May to October, the train steams in from Durango, as it has for more than a century. It actually steams. The engine burns coal and blows a steam whistle just like the first train did in 1882.

Odd, how history reverses itself. The tracks were built by the Denver & Rio Grande Railroad to carry ore out of the mountains.

Now they bring it in, a daily lode in the form of tourists and railroad buffs, five hundred strong, cameras clicking, coins jingling. They have come to ride the restored trains of the Durango & Silverton Narrow Gauge Railroad. It takes about four hours to travel 45 miles through some of the most rugged and scenic terrain in the Rockies. The Animas River tumbles blue and white in the bottom of its canyon, while craggy peaks draped with forest, wildflower meadows, and snowfields echo the high whistles of the steam engines. Best of all, there is no road in the canyon; it looks just as wild as it did a hundred years ago.

At Silverton, passengers walk among falling-down buildings, photograph tailing piles, and mentally reconstruct stamp mills from shattered ruins. They eat lunch at the French Bakery, the Grand Imperial Hotel, Zhivago's, or the Pickle Barrel, poke around in souvenir shops, and head back on the train to Durango. They could have driven their cars to Silverton in less time. They could have arrived without cinders in their hair. But people love the old smokey trains.

The locals are happy to play along. They plant ferns in ore buckets, hang rusted hand tools on walls, dress up in period costumes, and smile at visitors. In a manner of speaking, the people of Silverton are still miners, tapping a daily vein of nostalgia. Everyone enjoys the show, and as a train worker once pointed out, it's a lot safer than working underground.

It just took some resourceful thinking to keep Silverton alive. Mines might run dry but ideas never do. There's gold even in a sack of dirt if you know how to look for it.

Willard Clay

Decayed buildings and tailing ponds like these near Leadville, Colorado are often the only remnants of mining's boom days. Unlike ranchers, who tied their fortunes to the land, miners were transient opportunists. When the gold disappeared, so did they, taking only what they could carry.

Willard Clay

Mountain bluebells decorate the weathered pine planks of an abandoned building in the ghost town of St. Elmo, Colorado. Miners often lived in small towns scattered throughout the remote valleys of the Rockies. Others—and theirs are the more evocative ruins to find—led solitary lives far from human company, silently working their claims, living in tiny cabins and even in caves.

49

Willard Clay

Gingham curtains and preserved flowers hang in the windows of a house in the ghost town of Tincup, Colorado. Although the first gold seekers were men, women soon followed, softening the rough edges of rowdy mining camps but also proving themselves equal to men in fortitude and resourceful living. The Mountain States were the first in the country to grant full suffrage to women.

Tom Till

Ostler Peak, High Uintas Wilderness, Utah (*above*); Dillon Pinnacles rise above the waters of Blue Mesa Reservoir in the Curecanti National Recreation Area of Colorado (*right*). Colors in the West are often subtle, as the blush of grass stems gone to seed or the last touch of warm light on a craggy peak.

Willard Clay

52

I n the short mountain summer, plants must grow fast and bloom in a hurry. Everything seems to happen at once, as snowbanks melt and days grow warm. The result is a riotous flowering of columbine, Indian paintbrush, and others. The blossoms appear at the same time insects emerge to feed on nectar and, in the process, transfer pollen.

53

Willard Clay

Columbines, yellow balsam root, pink asters, and red Indian paintbrush form a perfect garden among lichen-covered boulders and lush green herbs. Nature is a skilled gardener, working with the tools of microclimate, moisture distribution, soil minerals, and sun exposure. The natural gardens of mountain meadows, complete with cascading streams and songbirds, surpass the efforts of any human gardener.

Larry Ulrich

54

Glacier lilies, looking like something from the *Arabian Nights*, blossom as snow melts. Among the earliest spring flowers in the valley, they can still be found in late summer in high meadows, emerging along the well-watered margins of shrinking snowfields.

Willard Clay

R ed Indian paintbrush are not the most honest citizens of the flower world. What look like blossoms are mostly colored bracts—modified leaves. The true flowers, hidden by the bracts, are unspectacular and easily overlooked. Besides being deceptive, paintbrush are root parasites; they produce only a portion of their own food, stealing the rest by tapping the roots of surrounding plants and proving that larceny can indeed have a pretty face.

Aspens and the Maroon Bells with fresh snow, White River National Forest, Colorado.

Larry Ulrich

CLOSING THE SEASON

Late fall. Recent snow has covered the high peaks of central Colorado.

"It looks deep up there," says my wife, Wendy. "How high do we go, anyway?"

I check the topographic map. "West Maroon Pass is over 12,400. We might be a bit too late in the season."

"I hope not."

So do I. I'd wanted to do this hiking trip for years—around the famous Maroon Bells—but I'd kept putting it off, thinking I should save it for October after the summer crowds had gone home.

The Maroon Bells area is one of the most popular places in the Rocky Mountains. Two nearly identical peaks, both over 14,000 feet, stand at the head of an idyllic glacial valley. Truly a perfect setting, it has crystalline lakes, tumbling creeks, wildflower meadows, a forest of mixed conifers and aspens, and spectacular peaks on three sides. All the grandeur of the Rockies in a single view.

Even people who have never seen Colorado know this valley. One of the most photographed views in the mountains, it has appeared on covers of numerous books and magazines. It lies just 10 miles from the city of Aspen and for that reason is crowded all summer. Yet even this late in the season, the parking area at the end of the road is a busy place. Families out for a drive stand with their backs to the peaks and pose for pictures. Bicyclists in stretch

suits labor up the road, stand briefly, sweating in the cool wind (everyone else is wearing jackets), then turn and start the wild ride back down. Three thousand feet to the valley bottom, coasting almost all the way.

For us, the climb begins here. We shoulder our packs and set off toward Crater Lake, a mile away and 500 feet above Maroon Lake. The trail ascends through brilliant golden aspen trees. Leaves flutter down in the light breeze, flurries of golden coins. I crush them beneath my boots. They smell of damp clay and autumn.

After a half hour, we reach Crater Lake. The view is even better than the one below. We gaze straight up the Maroon Bells. They are crazy with color: orange sedge, yellow aspens, red shrubby willows, deep green conifers, high sloping meadows in shades of brown and gray, purple cliffs, white snow, and a perfect blue sky. The air is warm enough that I could lie down in the crackling grass and fall asleep.

We'd better not if we want to get anywhere. Way at the head of the valley is a snow-covered wall. At its low point is West Maroon Pass. Our plan is to get as high as we can today without having to camp in the snow. It looks awfully remote.

"Let's go!" says Wendy.

The trail skirts Crater Lake at the base of the mountains. I can see the reason for the name, Maroon Bells. The sandstone and shale comprising these peaks are deep maroon in color. They are sediments worn off the ancestral Rockies that stood over Colorado some 300 million years ago.

Why is it, I wonder, that Mount Evans and Longs Peak, located farther east are both made of ancient crystalline granite, while the Maroon Bells, which are the same elevation, consist of younger stuff? There is granite in the Maroon Bells, but it's way under the surface. I chalk it up to the vagaries of geology. It would be boring to know it all.

Soon the trail becomes a thin track, no longer heavily used. It winds through deep groves of spruce and fir, big shady trees sheltering the morning's frost even late in the afternoon. Then it leads into the sun, where our feet slide on a thin layer of red mud.

In the talus fields, pikas (or rock rabbits) call from boulder-top perches. Red squirrels are busy in the conifers, chewing off pine cones, flinging them to the ground; they collect them in caches for winter food. Stopping for a rest, we sit against a sun-warmed boulder. Two gray jays hurry over from the forest to investigate. They are clearly used to getting handouts, but we give them nothing. A vole, short-tailed, gray, and about the size of a mouse, emerges from under a bush. It doesn't see me as it busily forages near my boot. A twitch of my ankle, and the furry bundle dives for cover.

A clatter of rocks makes me look high on the mountain, thinking bighorn sheep. I see no animals, even through binoculars. Rockfall is often caused by the simple action of freezing and thawing ice.

After three hours of walking, we reach timberline, about 11,400 feet, far higher than timberline at the Canadian end of the range. Looking back down the valley, I see a bright red mountain. Prospectors used to look for these colors; reds and yellows are often signs of mineralization. But not here. These mountains are just colorful sediments, sterile of gold and silver. And a good thing it is: We are better served by this place left unspoiled than we'd ever have been by the gold taken from it, had there been any to take. Wilderness areas like this survive largely because no one can find much of value in them. No gold, not much timber, too high, too snowy, the Maroon Bells Wilderness was ignored, left alone, and here we are breathing its clear fragrance.

The sun sets behind the ridge. Immediately we feel the cold.

It looks cold too, up here just below snowline. We quickly find a campsite on grass beside a ledge of smooth glaciated rock. While cooking supper, I scan the high meadows for animals; but the basin seems empty. Wendy finds the only wildlife when she dips a pot in the stream and collects a water strider. It races around the pot like a skater on an ice rink.

Day Two

Morning brings mare's tails in the sky, an ominous warning of approaching weather. We have four passes and nearly twenty miles to go. The fresh snow above our camp is not deep but a new storm could give us trouble. The mountains can be dangerous at this time of year. Winter might come hard and fast, dropping 3 or 4 feet of snow overnight. Some people carry snowshoes in October, just in case.

Not us. We've looked at the map and decided that from any point on this trail we can walk down a valley to a road. If snow forces us to do that, we will have a long hitchhike back to the car, but we won't be stranded.

Actually, we'd like the day to be a bit colder. The sun warms the trail, thawing the top layer of clay so that we struggle for footing. It feels as if we're walking on greased glass.

There is one good thing about the mud. It makes clear tracks. We find footprints of coyote, bobcat, deer, elk, and cloven hoofprints some 5 or 6 inches across—too big for an elk, but I can't imagine a moose wandering so far above timberline. "Maybe a cow," suggests Wendy. That seems even less likely, but it presents a nice image of a mountain-loving Hereford out for a stroll.

At West Maroon Pass the wind howls and threatens to push us over the cliff. Quickly, we leave it behind, following a slippery trail a thousand feet down through brown, crackling meadows. Treasure Mountain, huge and dome-shaped, looms across the valley to the west. We could walk that way, into the valley and over a low divide to the town of Crested Butte. Instead, we turn north toward Frigid Air Pass. In the warm sun, grasshoppers clatter away from my shadow; they won't be jumping much longer, not this late in the year.

Up to this point, we've made good time. But the other side of the pass faces northeast, and the slopes below are covered with snow—shallow snow that lies treacherously over sharp rocks and slippery grass. It takes us nearly an hour to work our way 400 feet down that difficult surface.

"It's taking lots longer than I thought it would."

"Can we make it all the way to Snowmass Lake tonight?" Wendy asks.

"If the trail wasn't so muddy, we could move faster."

The mud continues to be a problem. It clumps an inch thick on our boot soles, forcing us off the trail into the tussock grass. The hardest parts are where the trail cuts down steep embankments through dense willows. There's no alternative to walking on the trail then, so we skid awkwardly down the slick chutes.

But who's complaining? It's another beautiful day. Clouds are building in the southwest, but mostly the sky is sunny. I keep track of birds: three marsh hawks, a falcon, a snow-white ptarmigan, a twittering flight of purple finches. The trail drops from the open basin into a forest of big trees where sunlit glades alternate with deep green shadow and a mule deer, hearing us sliding along the trail, bounces off through the trees and partway up the willow-covered slope on the other side of the valley. Then she stands and watches, semaphore ears twitching, legs flexed and ready to run.

A mile farther, we come to the top of a cliff that cuts across the valley. The stream that we've been following falls abruptly 400 feet to a beaver pond at its base. Beyond, we can see a narrow, grass-covered valley glowing yellow between forested mountain slopes. The stream, having fallen so rapidly from the high basin, now spreads out and meanders from pool to pool.

It looks like trout water, and sure enough, I see a 14-inch brook trout while crossing the stream an hour later. I would just as soon stay in that meadow the rest of the day. But we are victims of a self-imposed agenda, and the weather looks worse every hour. Clouds have thickened. The wind has picked up. We know that Trail Rider Pass is still 2,000 feet above us and that our planned campsite at Snowmass Lake is another 1,400 feet down the other side. What if there's snow over there?

We should hurry but our feet are slow. Halfway to the pass, I wait fifteen minutes for Wendy to catch up. She looks tired. "Maybe we can go partway," I suggest.

"I'd hate to be stuck on this side if it snows," she says.

She's right. The clouds are now a solid gray sheet, driven by a hard southwest wind. We plug on, climbing to a tiny lake set in a rolling meadow 700 feet below the pass. We are again tempted to stop.

"It's crazy to pass up such a perfect campsite," I say. Just then a strong, icy gust roars up the valley, and this place suddenly seems inhospitable. In July, no doubt, wildflowers carpet this little meadow, and hikers relaxing in the shade of the few wind-stunted trees listen for hummingbirds. Today, summer seems like a half-remembered dream, something that couldn't really have happened. Up here, at timberline, snow and ice are the overwhelming facts of life—and death. We decide to push on. It's comforting to know that from the other side of Trail Rider Pass, if it snows heavily, we can go out on a different trail, avoiding Buckskin Pass (the last of four) and still end up in Aspen Valley.

We reach the pass and start down; only 600 feet below the pass, in fading light, well shy of Snowmass Lake, our enthusiasm runs out. The elevation is 11,800 feet, mighty high for late October. But we have no choice. Tired as we are, continuing down the snow-covered trail in the dark would be riskier than staying high, even if it does storm. Perching the tent on the brink of a cliff that drops 800 feet to the dark, rock-rimmed waters of the lake, we hurriedly fix supper and climb into our sleeping bags. Wind tears at the nylon. I can hear each gust roaring down the valley. The first snow squall arrives as I drift off to sleep.

Day Three

At first light, I peer out at a white world. Both of us slept poorly, listening to the sound of snow avalanching off the roof of the tent, wondering how deep it was getting outside. We could walk through two feet of snow if necessary. If it was downhill. If we had to.

In the morning, I'm relieved to see that it's only 5 inches deep. But more snow is falling. The mountains are invisible. We pack quickly and move down the trail, hunching our shoulders against the wind. There is one more pass, Buckskin, three hours away. Like the others, it is 12,400 feet high. Another geologic puzzle: Why are all four passes on this circle the same elevation?

At first we hurry, thinking the longer it takes us to reach the pass, the deeper the snow will be. But then, as we enter dense forest in the valley bottom, the clouds lift somewhat. It stops snowing. Spotlights of sun hit the summits of Snowmass and Hagerman peaks. We see them from scattered meadows as we climb the grade to Buckskin Pass, and although the wind is still strong and the temperature below freezing, I know we have nothing to worry about from the weather.

Marginal times like these, when you probably shouldn't be outdoors, are often the most rewarding. We walk easily, exhilarated by the power of mountain weather and the joy of being out in it. As we climb, snow squalls wash over the ridges. Mountains disappear, then burst from veils of cloud, glittering in patches of sunlight. We stop repeatedly and stare at one of the Rocky Mountains' most scenic areas in the year's most spectacular weather.

One look at Wendy's face and I know how she feels.

"Too bad you don't like mountains," I say.

She smiles. "I could be at home watching TV and eating bonbons." It's an old joke of ours.

Almost too soon, we arrive at Buckskin Pass. The wind batters us from one side, then the other. Nonetheless, we linger for half an hour, taking in the view, trying to trace the way we came that morning. Having walked through all that massive scenery, having measured the miles with our feet, we have a feeling for the place that we could get in no other way.

Finally, shivering from cold, we turn and head down. Below, hidden by an intervening ridge, lies Crater Lake where we started this circle. Across the valley, the vast wall of 14,018-foot Pyramid

Peak slips in and out of sight as snowstorms cruise the valley. From here, we are looking down on them.

At the treeline, we stop for lunch. A woman in shorts and running shoes comes trotting up the trail. Wendy and I are bundled in parkas and insulated pants, with snow gaiters over our boots.

"Hi!" says the jogger. "Is it snowing on the pass?"

"Yes, it is. We were cold up there."

"Well, it's a lot warmer down below."

She runs on up the trail, looking fitter than we feel. We move slowly down, below the snow, into the forest. The air is much warmer, and I'm just feeling as if we've put the rugged country behind us when we meet two men on their way up. Neither one carries a pack but they eye us with suspicion.

"Where've you been?" one of them asks.

Wendy tells him we've made a circle trip around the Maroon Bells.

"Are you carrying your snowshoes?"

"No," says Wendy. "Just walking shoes."

The man looks knowingly at his companion. "Happens every year. Unprepared people get in trouble." They leave, shaking their heads. I wonder what they will say to the woman in shorts.

An hour later, back at the car, I see that the Maroon Bells are almost entirely obscured by a wicked-looking black cloud. It is snowing again on the heights, piling up, drifting, obscuring our footprints.

Late October really is the end of the season.

61

Willard Clay

Well after snow has melted and meadows have turned green, summer snowbanks remain. This one, a concentration of snow caused by wind drifting in winter, is tinted by a type of red algae that thrives in granular summer snow, giving it the common name of watermelon snow.

62

Willard Clay

The Black Canyon of the Gunnison cuts through some of the oldest rock in North America—Precambrian gneiss about 2 billion years old. This same ancient basement rock underlies most of the continent, but it is exposed only rarely, in places like the bottom of the Grand Canyon and mountain cliffs around Rocky Mountain National Park, Colorado.

Willard Clay

63

Waterfalls in the Elk Mountains of Colorado. In the long run, water is the most precious commodity in the Rockies. An average of 17 inches of water falls on the West each year—about half the rainfall that occurs in Illinois—but this is a rough figure. Some places get far less than that. The mountains and forests, because they hold snow and groundwater well into summer, are important natural reservoirs.

Willard Clay

The Big Thompson River flows gently through Moraine Park in Rocky Mountain National Park. The word *park* has a double meaning. It can refer to an open, relatively flat place in the mountains; hence the Colorado Rockies claim Estes Park, Moraine Park, and the trio of North, South, and Middle parks. Farther north, people call similar valleys *holes*, as in Jackson Hole and Pierre's Hole.

65

Willard Clay

Yellow leaves lie like gold coins on the floor of an aspen forest in Rocky Mountain National Park. Fall colors have been in the leaves all year long. They become visible, however, with the approach of cold weather, when the plants break down the green chlorophyll and absorb the nutrients, thus gradually revealing bright carotenoid pigments.

66

Pat O'Hara

Beneath Hallet Peak in Rocky Mountain National Park, slopes are covered by aspens turning yellow. Autumn begins at high altitudes. As early as late August, you can see a warning flash of gold from some high aspen grove. By mid-September, the entire slope is brilliant with various shades of yellow.

Willard Clay

For some reason, the second week of September is often an unsettled time when storms and wet snow fall on green leaves and the last wildflowers of summer.

68

Larry Ulrich

The storms of early September usually give way to an extended and beautiful Indian summer when days are warm but nights are cold and crisp. Here, at Mount Timpanogos in Utah's Wasatch Range, gambel oak, aspens, and various shrubs combine in an exuberant display.

Larry Ullrich

69

A spens on the Wasatch Plateau have lost many of their lower leaves. Enhancing the colors of autumn, anthocyanin pigments are produced by converting the last sugar in leaves before they die. The longer leaves survive in the fall, the brighter they become. The show ends with a killing frost or a strong wind that strips the last leaves from naked branches.

Warren Peak in the Anaconda Pintler Mountains, Montana.

PART TWO
HOT SPRINGS & WILD RIVERS

The Teton Range, Wyoming.

THE MIDDLE ROCKIES

When Lewis and Clark set off on their voyage of discovery, they had a simple idea: to ascend the Missouri River to its headwaters, carry their boats over the Divide, and float down to the Pacific Ocean more or less the way explorers in the East had crossed the Appalachians and floated down the Ohio and Mississippi rivers to the Gulf of Mexico.

It didn't work. The Rockies weren't the Appalachians. They were much higher, much wider, and much more rugged. Rivers didn't flow through the Rockies, they crashed wildly down through canyons with walls often too steep even for foot trails.

By the time Lewis and Clark and their men had reached the headwaters of the Missouri, at what is now the border between southwest Montana and Idaho, they had already wasted a huge amount of time trying to stick with their plan. Almost two months earlier, they had arrived at Great Falls, Montana, portaged their boats (a 24-day job), and journeyed slowly up the Missouri, trying to guess which of various tributaries was the most likely to follow. With the help of the young Shoshone woman Sacajawea, they had chosen the Beaverhead River. As they had hoped, the Beaverhead led them to the Divide where they entered the Pacific drainage. Better yet, the first western slope people they met were Shoshone Indians, notably Sacajawea's brother Cameahwait.

That was the good news. The bad news was that they were still about 800 miles from the ocean, facing one of the most difficult, convoluted landscapes in America—the mountains of central Idaho. Forget the river, advised Cameahwait, you'll have to go back over the Divide and north to the Nez Percé Trail, the Lolo Trail. And anyway, what are you crazy white men doing way down here? You should have traded your boats for horses back at Great Falls where the trail begins! Would have saved all kinds of trouble.

The great captains must have felt a bit like city boys from Boston lost on the back roads of Maine: Is this the way to Bangor?

If you look at a highway map of the West, the problem becomes clear. You still can't drive through the middle of Idaho. Interstate 80 shoots across southern Wyoming through the Great Divide Basin, over the Continental Divide, and down to Salt Lake City, entirely avoiding the really rugged country. The road stays high, the wind blows like the devil, not much grows up there but despite all that, the landscape is open. Along much of Wyoming's I-80, you can't see any mountains. About 300 miles north, another interstate, I-90, cuts easily across Montana until it reaches Three Forks, where mountainous terrain forces the highway northwest to cross the Divide way up near Coeur D'Alene, Idaho.

As for the Nez Percé Trail, it followed a ridge above the Lochsa River canyon. It may have been the only feasible route west, but that didn't make it easy. Lewis and Clark found the going extremely difficult and disheartening. It took highway engineers until 1962 to build a road along the Lochsa, an arduous job itself.

Mountain man Jim Bridger, the first non-Indian to thoroughly explore the middle Rockies, boasted that you could set him down anywhere in the region and he'd know where he was. The country remains wild and unaltered enough that Bridger could probably do the same thing today—unless you set him down in the middle of a city like Pocatello, Idaho, in which case he'd be "powerful confused." Back in Bridger's day, there was nothing like a city for a thousand miles, not a house, not a fence, not a railroad, not a mining town, not a ranch, and sure as blazes not an interstate highway. Imagine what he'd think, riding through some kind of Wild West *Twilight Zone* and coming across I-80 in the middle of Wyoming. It would happen at dusk. He'd be weary, not paying attention, and suddenly his horse would be standing on this strange smooth strip of stone. What the Bejasus? Jim gets down to look at it more closely. He hears a distant throbbing roar. What in tarnation is that?

We hope he gets off the pavement when the trucker blows his horn. Damn fool with his horse in the middle of the road! Waving a rifle!

Bridger no doubt would spin some tall tales over that one. But one thing would not surprise him, once he learned what highways were about. He would nod knowingly about the choice of route. Whether trapper, wagon boss, or highway engineer, it was best not to argue with the shape of the country.

In fact, men like Bridger established the first wagon roads across the Rockies. When the fur trade died, many trappers stayed on in the mountains as guides for overland settlers. Before he went back to die in Missouri, Bridger operated a trading post and supply house along the Oregon Trail, sort of the first truck stop in the Mountain West.

The middle Rockies divide neatly in two parts on either side of the Continental Divide—one in Idaho, the other mostly in Wyoming with some of southwestern Montana. The Idaho portion occupies the center of the state, bounded on the south and west by the Snake River and on the north by the low, forested outlyers of Canada's Columbia Mountains. Some of Idaho's mountains are spectacular—for example, the Sawtooths, the Pioneers, and the Bitterroots—but because most of the region is a convoluted labyrinth of canyons and sharp twisting ridges, it seems best defined by the way water flows through it, in other words, by its rivers: in Idaho, the Selway, the Lochsa, the Clearwater, the Payette, and most important, the Salmon; in Montana, the various streams comprising the Missouri River headwaters.

Idaho rivers flow every which way, twisting around on themselves in an entirely unpredictable and confusing manner. Mapmakers have tried making sense of the puzzle by attaching directional names like South Fork and North Fork to the various tributary streams. That makes sense until you realize that the south fork of some river begins north of the north fork; or when you encounter the East Fork of the Lake Fork of the North Fork of the Payette River, and you wish they had just called it something simple like Columbine Creek. Never mind trying to make sense of central Idaho. The pleasure of the place comes from its gobbledygook geography.

The second part of this region takes up most of Wyoming and southwest Montana, dominated by a complex of high country centered on the Yellowstone Plateau. Attention here shifts naturally from rivers to mountains. Ranges comprise distinct landmarks rising above broad valleys. You watch them for miles as you drive the area's highways, becoming familiar with the shape of their summits against the sky. Like city skylines with characteristic buildings, each range has its own profile: the Winds, the Bighorns, the Tetons, the Absaroka, the Crazies, the Tobacco Roots, and the Bridgers. Once you learn the profiles, you could wake up suddenly almost anywhere in the region and—like Bridger—know where you were.

Most of the time you'd be in ranch country or on federal land. If you took away all the territory used for raising cattle, the country would be a lot smaller. If you then removed all the national forests, national parks, wilderness areas, wildlife refuges, and federal rangeland, you'd be left with something about the size of New York's Central Park. Or so it seems.

The middle Rockies owe their existence primarily to volcanism. Central Idaho rests upon an enormous batholith, a body of igneous rock that squeezed its way between sedimentary layers 60 to 90 million years ago without breaking the surface. You could think of it as a volcanic blister covering 14,000 square miles. Subsequent erosion exposed the hardened batholith, revealing the crazy topography we see today. Just to the south, the Snake River Plain is covered with lava flows, the most recent ones only 2 million years old. And obviously, considering its thermal activity, the Yellowstone Plateau remains an active hot spot, including several cataclysmic eruptions that quite literally blew the surface off the park—plants, rocks, trees, animals, lakes, the whole works.

On the other hand, many of the area mountains are fault-block mountains, revealing ancient basement rock like that of Longs Peak in Colorado. These include nearly every range in Wyoming outside of Yellowstone: the Tetons, the Winds, the Snowy Range, the Bighorns. The same holds true for southwest Montana.

You might expect such old-rock mountains to contain rich lodes. In fact, the central Rockies have produced comparatively little in the way of precious metals. Virginia City, Montana grew up beside one of the richest placer strikes of all, but quickly faded. South Pass, Wyoming saw brief activity yielding modest amounts of gold. Scattered locations throughout central Idaho prospered for a few years before being abandoned. There were others, some of significant size including Helena and Orofino, but these were on the edge of the Rockies, not in the heart of the mountains like Colorado's Aspen or Telluride. And in none of them did mining last long enough to dominate the local economy for long.

Except, of course, in Butte, Montana, where copper was king for nearly a century. Some 17 billion pounds of copper were extracted from the surrounding hills, the largest mine being the Berkeley Pit, an enormous colorful crater on the edge of the city's business district. Butte once touted itself as the most cosmopolitan city between St. Louis and San Francisco. In the 1920s, its population hit a peak of over 100,000. Today the mines are closed and Butte, much diminished from its heyday, is a quieter, some say more enjoyable, city of about 30,000.

In general, the middle Rockies were spared from the frenzied hubbub of surrounding districts. The flood tides of a growing nation flowed elsewhere. The Oregon Trail, heavy with westward-bound settlers, skirted just south of the area. The big gold and

silver discoveries of interior British Columbia and the Idaho panhandle drew prospectors to the north. Until 1871, when the first official survey party had a look at the place, the wonders of Yellowstone were dismissed as incredible fantasies.

It was different in Colorado, where mining provided the money and incentive for an astonishing network of railroads and other industries. Not even timber companies showed much interest in the middle Rockies, once they realized that the region's forests grew relatively small trees—predominantly lodgepole pines, which are nice for building log cabins but too small for sawlogs. Much better were the forests of northern Idaho and Montana—and, of course, the coastal states. Wetter and lower, they yielded the beautiful stands of western red cedar, hemlock, Douglas fir, and western white pine coveted by loggers.

A century ago, the only industry the central Rockies were really good for was ranching and, in limited areas, farming. Transport services grew in importance as highways were built. Tourism increased with easier transport, most rapidly in recent decades. Although gold and silver mining never made it big, there is significant mining of coal, uranium, soda ash, bentonite, oil, and gas (mostly in areas peripheral to the mountains) and some timber cutting. Even so, the regional population remains small. Wyoming ranks fiftieth in the nation. There are fewer people in its 97,914 square miles than in lower Manhattan. The situation in Montana is about the same; it ranks fourth in size but forty-fourth in population. The biggest town in central Idaho is Salmon with about 3,300 people. They like it just fine, thank you. They sure don't worry about hitting people with their elbows.

Ask a hundred local people to name their favorite spot in the central Rockies, and you'll get a hundred different answers. They won't all name famous places either. For instance, there is an alpine basin in the Wind River Range called the Cirque of the Towers that ranks among the most beautiful settings in North America. Above a sparkling body of water named Lonesome Lake rises a series of pinnacles called Pingora, Shark's Nose, Wolf Jaw, and such. Made of glacially polished granite, they soar against the early morning sky, rivaling better-known peaks like the Tetons or the Sawtooths. To get there you must walk or ride a horse, which is fitting and proper. The effort of getting there has much to do with how long and how vividly one remembers that exquisite alpine gem.

Or consider Rosebud Lake, in Montana, at the base of the stunning Beartooth escarpment. You can drive your car there, camp in a national forest campground, and gaze upward at walls that rival those of Yosemite Valley in California. The campgrounds on the other side of the Beartooth Range, in Yellowstone, are choked all summer by people looking for the sort of spectacular tranquility so easily found at unrenowned lakes like Rosebud.

Places like these are the rule, not the exception. There are, after all, quite a few Rocky Mountains outside the national parks, and not one of them can be dismissed as boring, trivial, mundane, or tiresome on the eyes. Quite the contrary, the real gems are the ones most often overlooked, the ones you find on your own and take to heart for personal reasons.

This is not to say that the celebrated landscapes are less than wonderful. Who can forget the surging crest of the Teton Range viewed on an evening in July? Yellowstone's Upper Geyser Basin (all of it, not just Old Faithful) works continuous wonder with shifting vapors. The Grand Canyon of the Yellowstone River, colored yellow, red, brown, even shades of green, has delighted observers since before Thomas Moran painted the first watercolor of it.

The list of scenic highlights, both famous and obscure, runs long. In Wyoming, there is Flaming Gorge on the Green River, mighty Tensleep Canyon in the Bighorn Range, the Snowy Range near Laramie, the stark but haunting Great Divide Basin, where wild horses run with pronghorn antelope. At South Pass, hard beneath the southern flank of the Wind River Range, you can see the parallel ruts from wagon trains that passed a century ago.

In Idaho, Redfish Lake and the Sawtooth Range epitomize the charms of alpine landscape, completely different from the forbidding lava flows at Craters of the Moon National Monument. There is the towering Bitterroot Range, the fog-shrouded Lochsa River Valley, the brooding vastness of the River of No Return Wilderness, and the mile-deep gash of Hells Canyon.

In southwest Montana the mountains are farther apart. The landscape becomes more spacious, the valleys wider, the scenery easy on the eyes. Enough cannot be said about the beauty of the Big Hole Valley; in fact people who know it well tend to clam up for fear of attracting attention. Far more people have seen the gorgeous view from State Highway 287 above Ennis, looking across the Madison River at Sphinx Peak, while literally millions are familiar with a place rightly called Paradise Valley on the road to Yellowstone from Livingston. Southwest Montana is good for the soul. Drive any of its secondary roads, and your heart will rest content for a few days afterward. If you doubt this, take the road between Three Forks and Hebgen Reservoir on a July evening when mayflies are rising from the Madison River and meadowlarks are perched on every tenth fencepost. Driving slowly with open windows, you can smell the freshly cut hay.

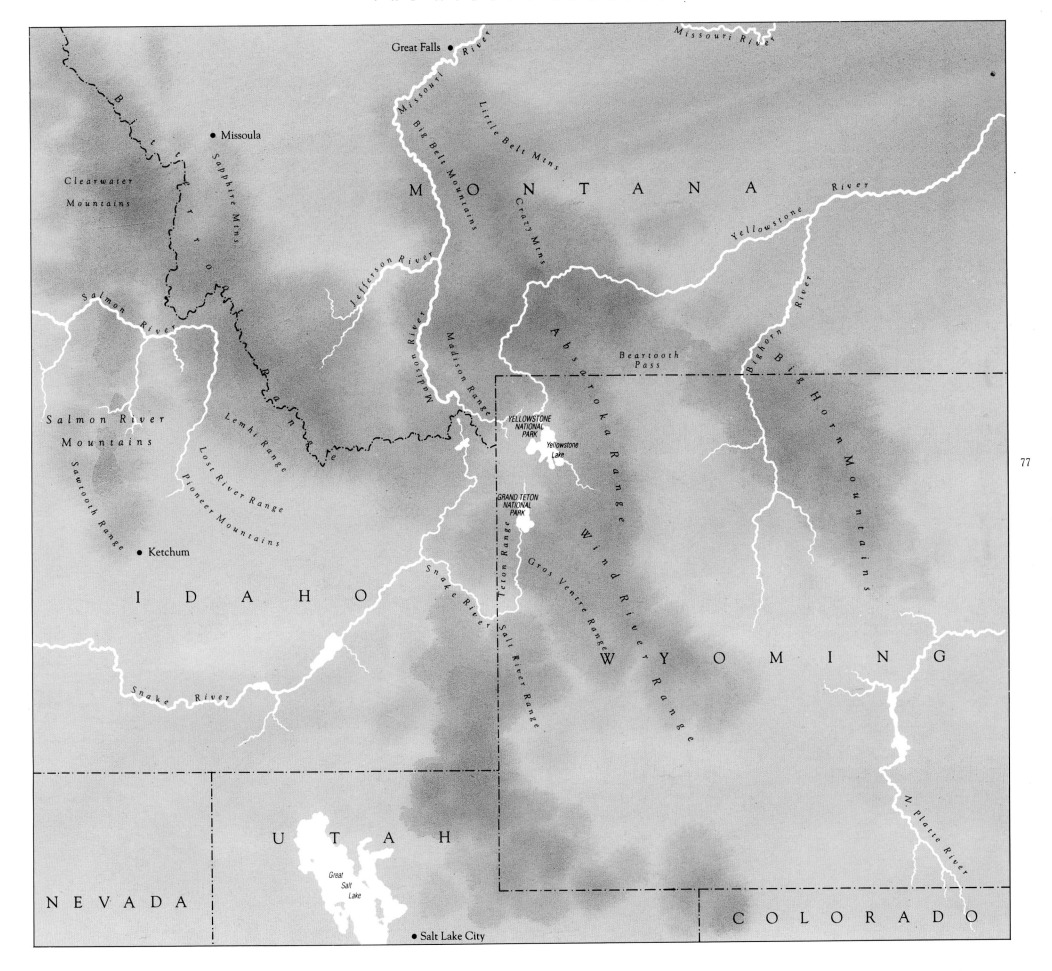

Great Falls ●

● Missoula

Clearwater
Mountains

Salmon River

Salmon River
Mountains

Sawtooth Range

● Ketchum

Sapphire Mtns

Lemhi Range

Lost River Range

Pioneer Mountains

I D A H O

Snake River

Snake River

Missouri River

M O N T A N A

Big Belt Mountains

Little Belt Mtns

Crazy Mtns

Jefferson River

Madison River

Madison Range

Yellowstone River

River

Absaroka Range

Beartooth
Pass

YELLOWSTONE
NATIONAL
PARK

Yellowstone
Lake

GRAND TETON
NATIONAL
PARK

Teton Range

Gros Ventre Range

Wind River Range

Salt River Range

W Y O M I N G

Bighorn River

Big Horn Mountains

Missouri River

N E V A D A

U T A H

Great
Salt
Lake

● Salt Lake City

C O L O R A D O

N. Platte River

77

Pat O'Hara

78

Many people consider the Tetons to be the consummate expression of mountain geography. Rising some 7,000 vertical feet above the valley floor, they are classic fault-block mountains; that is, an enormous block of stone was tilted above the surrounding land, resulting in a grand escarpment on the east side and a more gradual incline on the west.

Pat O'Hara

Deep canyons cut into the Tetons give the impression that they are one amazingly sharp wall. Actually, numerous meadows and lakes are found among the high crags. Some of these lakes remain frozen well into July.

80

Pat O'Hara

Cold weather never really leaves the highest summits of the Tetons, where glaciers and snowfields survive throughout the year, and snow can fall in July. Warm weather comes through like a tourist, staying a brief two months, then abandons the mountains once more to the spectacular arctic world of winter.

Pat O'Hara

Pat O'Hara

Tom Till

Jackson Hole, the valley east of the Tetons, is one of the coldest places in the Rockies. On January nights, when there is no wind and the sky is clear, intense cold settles into low areas along the Snake River. By morning, trees are delicately coated with mist rising from the river. Winter lows of 30 degrees below zero are not remarkable. People don't start talking about it until the air hits minus 50.

83

Pat O'Hara

84

Par O'Hara

Indian paintbrush, lupine, bistort, and buttercups grace an alpine basin in the Wind River Range of Wyoming. Reachable only by trail, places like this make the effort of even short walks worthwhile.

Pat O'Hara

Pat O'Hara

Mountain bluebells grow among yellow senecio (*left*) and columbine (*right*). All prefer moist soil, especially the columbines, which produce their densest blossoms where melting snow or springwater soak the earth. Blue columbine is the state flower of Colorado; farther north, the flower grows less blue—even shading to yellow or white.

Pat O'Hara

Once charred by fire, a venerable whitebark pine snag has been scoured by wind
and weather until it resembles the clean, glacially polished lines of the pinnacles
in the Wind River Range's Cirque of the Towers in Wyoming.

Pat O'Hara

I sland Lake, reflecting Harrower Peak, lies on the west slope of the Wind River Range. The lake is free of ice for less than three months each year. Because these mountains consist of hard granite polished by glaciers, the range exhibits smooth exposed rock slopes, little vegetation, and many frigid lakes.

Titcomb Basin in the Wind River Range, Wyoming.

MOUNTAIN LEGENDS

It was the summer of 1807. John Colter and a man named Potts were setting beaver traps from a canoe. They were in a small creek near Three Forks of the Missouri River. Blackfeet country. Present-day Montana. They heard a rumble. "What's that?" said Colter.

"Buffalo," said Potts.

Wrong. It was Blackfeet Indians, five or six hundred of them, on horseback, crowding the bank, bows drawn, laughing at this delightful discovery. Colter and Potts were floating ducks.

The Indians waved them to shore. Colter climbed out. An Indian grabbed Potts's rifle. Colter snatched it back and handed it to Potts, who pushed off in the canoe. "Don't move!" said Colter. An arrow hit Potts. Colter urged him back to shore, "You can't escape!" But Potts had apparently made a quick decision regarding the manner of his death. No torture for him. He raised his rifle and fired on the Blackfeet. Instantly, he was riddled with arrows.

Colter still thought of survival, even as they stripped him naked and argued over how to kill him. "Are you a fast runner?" asked a chief. "No. I ride horses," said Colter. Actually, he was a pretty good runner, especially if several hundred Blackfeet provided a good reason to go fast. They gave him a short head start, just to enjoy the sight of his pink rump going off through the prickly pear cactus and sagebrush.

The Jefferson River was 6 miles away. Colter had no real hope of finding refuge there, but at least it was something to run for. He ran with all his heart. A mile from the river, he glanced back. Only one man, armed with a spear, was gaining on him. Desperate, Colter spun to confront the Indian, who stumbled in surprise. Grabbing the spear, Colter stabbed his opponent and continued his wild dash to the river.

Now the other Blackfeet were really mad. They came roaring up to the riverbank. But Colter was gone, hiding underwater beneath a logjam. Blackfeet swarmed along the river's edge, and probed the logjam. Colter could see their shadows moving above him and heard their angry voices. He worried that they might torch the driftwood, but they didn't.

That night, he set off downriver, swimming for a while, then walking, stark naked. It took him seven days to reach Fort Lisa at the junction of the Bighorn and Yellowstone rivers. He walked in with nothing but his skin and a good story.

That's how Colter told it. He had been with Lewis and Clark to the Pacific, but had decided to remain in the mountains when the expedition headed east. He is considered to be the first of that legendary breed, the mountain men. Among them were some of the most enduring characters of the Old West—familiar names like Jim Bridger, Tom Fitzpatrick, Jedediah Smith, Kit Carson,

Bill Sublette, Joe Meek, Osborne Russell, and others.

Their era was a short one. Despite the activities of a few pioneers like Colter, the mountain fur trade did not really begin until the early 1820s, when William Ashley and Andrew Henry organized the Rocky Mountain Fur Company. Instead of building trading posts at strategic locations and buying furs from the Indians (the method of Canada's Hudson's Bay Company), Ashley and Henry hired young men to do the trapping. They were paid not by the number of beaver they trapped, but by the season. Therefore, if they did well, the profits for Ashley and Henry—and for other companies that soon joined the business—could be enormous.

The best of the trappers, seeing the potential and having developed a taste for the magnificent scenery and freedom of mountain life, took off on their own, leaving behind the organization and salaries of the big companies. They called themselves "free trappers" and traveled when and where they pleased, in loosely organized groups or completely alone. They became very good at living in the mountains.

There were never very many. David Lavender, in his book, *The Rockies*, estimates no more than 1,000 total. Of those, at least 281 were killed by Indians and natural hazards. It was a hard life, but apparently one they loved.

Once each year they would rendezvous at an agreed-on location, where they would sell their furs to the clerks and owners of the various competing companies. They rarely took money for the pelts. Instead, they exchanged furs for the tools of their trade—horses, rifles, powder, lead, beaver traps, blankets, knives—and for a few minimal comforts like coffee, flour, cotton cloth, and trinkets for their Indian wives. Anything left after that went for party supplies—cheap watered alcohol made to faintly resemble whisky. It was the social event of the year.

By the late 1830s, after less than two decades, the party was nearly over. The inexhaustible supply of beaver had vanished. Pelts were scarce and the demand for them had plummeted in the face of changing European fashion. Beaver hats were out; silk hats were in.

The mountain men gave up on beaver trapping. They wandered off to become trail guides, army scouts, buffalo hunters, farmers, or legends. One of the legends was Jim Bridger, who died on a Missouri farm in 1881, blind and poor. Reportedly, he yearned for the Rockies, saying, "I wish I war back thar among the mountains agin. A man can see so much farther in that country."

At the peak of his powers, Bridger had been the leader of a sizeable nomadic village: 240 free trappers with their Indian wives, their children, their horses, and other belongings looked to "Old Gabe" in the same way their native neighbors looked to their chiefs for guidance and wise counsel. He knew the Rockies like no man before him, and perhaps like no one since. He had seen the country in its pristine youth. Spring winds had stirred his blood; autumn frost had thickened it. He had seen the endless bison herds, the great Plains Indian camps, and the Blackfeet at the height of their powers. He had ridden thousands of miles without seeing a building or encountering a fence. He knew the sweep of the plains, the crash of thunder among the summits.

How did he ever go back to rural Missouri?

One of the better personal accounts to come from that era is Osborne Russell's. He gave us a glimpse into the reasons he loved the life, in a description of his favorite mountain valley:

I almost wished I could spend the remainder of my days in a place like this where happiness and contentment seemed to reign in wild romantic splendor surrounded by majestic battlements which seemed to support the heavens and shut out all hostile intruders.

He loved the place, adding later:

There is something in the wild romantic scenery of this valley which I cannot, nor will I, attempt to describe but the impressions made upon my mind while gazing from a high eminence on the surrounding landscape one evening as the sun was gently gliding behind the western mountain and casting its gigantic shadows across the vale were such as time can never efface from my memory.

The objective history of the Rocky Mountain fur trade, although it includes the mountain men as essential characters, is primarily a story of dealings between rival companies and politicians. It involves business decisions, legal maneuvers, the ethics of profit—in other words, free enterprise American-style.

But the mountain men were from the opposite side of the moon, philosophically speaking. Happier holed up for the winter in a Crow Indian village than in any city, they were as ornery and independent a bunch of misfits as the United States has ever seen—men in search of a frontier, of a social margin where they could be free to exercise their independence.

They certainly weren't businessmen, although a few tried to be. And for a bunch of future legends, they had very little skill or inclination for self-promotion. Their real feelings about themselves are reflected by the stories they told and retold, like the escape of John Colter. However the truth might have been stretched, these are the tales that meant the most to those who lived the trapping life. Mostly they deal with heroic, independent acts, the lone man prevailing, and laughing, in the face of adversity. A few have become classics, woven into the permanent mythology of the West. As such, they are more interesting and perhaps nearer to the truth of the times than the unadorned facts of objective history.

We have room here for only a few, but they are doozies.

Hugh Glass was hunting in dense brush when he ran into a grizzly bear with cubs. It was bad news delivered fast. The bear knocked him down, mauled him, and took a bite out of him. His friends killed the bear, but it looked like the end for old Glass. No man could survive such terrible wounds.

Nervous about Indians, no one wanted to stick around waiting for Glass to die. Finally the men passed a hat and offered eighty dollars as a reward. Two men, the greenhorn Jim Bridger and a guy named Fitzgerald, agreed to stay, if only to bury Glass.

Days later, Glass was apparently not recovering, but he remained too stubborn to die. Bridger and Fitzgerald were in a panic, worrying about Indians. They cleared out, taking Glass's rifle and other valuables. They weren't thieves, but how could they explain having left those things with a dead man? Surely he was dead.

Not so. Glass regained consciousness, dragged himself to a spring, and ate berries and roots until he felt ready to travel. Fort Kiowa was 100 miles away. He couldn't stand. He crawled on his elbows, driven by thoughts of revenge on those who had abandoned him. Partway there, he found wolves on a freshly killed buffalo calf. He beat off the wolves and claimed the prize and thus fortified somehow managed to reach Fort Kiowa.

That alone would have made him a legend. But there's more. At the fort, he hitched a ride with a boat headed upriver. Nice ride, but too slow. Glass decided to walk ahead of the boat across a bend in the river. The next day, all the men in the boat died in an Aricara Indian ambush. Nor was Glass safe. Within sight of his destination, Tilton's Fort, he was spotted by Aricaras, who gave chase. Glass hobbled desperately, without hope. Suddenly, two friendly Mandan Indians on horseback came roaring in, swept him up, and carried him to safety in the fort.

He left that night, walking for thirty-eight days to the mouth of the Bighorn River where he found his former friends. It was New Year's Eve. They thought they were seeing a ghost. In a sense they were. Bridger was mortified and repentant, and Glass forgave him the sins of youth. But he still wanted Fitzgerald, and Fitzgerald had gone back downriver.

So Glass turned around and traveled with four companions, overland across Wyoming to the Platte River. They built a boat of buffalo skins and floated until a band of Aricaras beckoned them to shore. Glass knew the chief; he had spent a whole winter with him. "It's all right," he told his pals.

Wrong again. The friendly meeting turned into another wild footrace. Glass saved himself while two of his friends were killed. The other two escaped and disappeared. Glass made for Fort Kiowa alone, upright this time and he had his knife.

From Fort Kiowa he continued to Fort Atkinson. There he found Fitzgerald, who must have stood with his mouth hanging open. But if Glass had seriously planned revenge, he now had to change his mind. Fitzgerald had joined the army and was protected by his uniform. At least Glass got his rifle back.

Joe Meek had a funnier view of grizzlies. He and his pal Hawkins saw a bear—a huge one, of course—across the river. They shot it and thought it was dead. Stripping naked except for knives and belts, they swam across to collect a trophy. Surprise! The grizzly, still alive, attacked:

Then you ought to have seen two naked men run! It war a race for life, and a close one, too. But we made the river first . . . Overboard we went, the bar after us. The current war very strong, and the bar war about half way between Hawkins and me. Hawkins war trying to swim down stream faster than the current war carrying the bar, and I war trying to hold back. You can reckon that I swam! Every moment I felt myself being washed into the yawning jaws of the mighty beast, whose head war up the stream and his eyes on me . . . Hawkins war the first to make the shore, unknown to the bar, whose head war still up stream; and he set up such a whooping and yelling that the bar landed too, but on the opposite side. I made haste to follow Hawkins . . . and then we traveled back a mile and more to whar our mules war left—a bar on one side of the river, and two bares on the other! (Frances Fuller Victor, River of the West, *page 91)*

Mike Fink was a hell of a shot, and a drinker and a fighter. They called him "King of the Keelboats." Five foot nine, 180 pounds, a square brawny man, he boasted of having once shot the tails off pigs from a moving boat.

He had two friends named Carpenter and Talbot. Carpenter and Fink often did a little trick. It went like this: One would put a cup of whisky on his head and stand still; the other would shoot it off. Then they would change places and do it again. More than a trick, it was a mutual display of marksmanship and trust. As the story goes, one time they quarreled. Fink suggested they make up and shoot the cup to prove their friendship. Carpenter agreed, but told others in the group that he thought Fink meant to shoot him. He made a will giving everything to Talbot and stood up with the cup on his head. Fink took aim, saying, "Now don't shake and spill the whisky," and proceeded to shoot Carpenter through the forehead. Fink stood for a moment, staring at his fallen friend. "You spilled the whisky!" was all he had to offer as an epitaph.

Talbot, some months later, shot Fink to death. But life was hard for all mountain men, and how you died was just a matter of time and place. Talbot eventually drowned in the Teton River.

Osborne Russell, who survived long enough to move to Oregon and write his fine book *Journal of a Trapper*, told this one: He and his companion White are in their camp near Yellowstone Lake when a band of Blackfeet jump them. They run for it. White gets an arrow in his hip. He yanks it out and keeps running. Russell gets shot in the hip too. Then in the thigh. The second arrow fells him; he drags himself into a pile of logs where White has taken refuge. The Blackfeet, unable to find them, loot the camp and leave.

After a long wait, the two men struggle to the lakeshore, wounded and empty-handed. White's nerve fails. Russell gives him hell. "You son of a rich man. You sissy!"

The next day, Russell needs crutches to move. White is better. They move off and run into another member of their trapping brigade. He has a bag of salt, the only thing the Blackfeet left behind. Russell washes his wound with the salt, then applies beaver oil.

Three days they travel. It pours rain. By the fourth day, Russell walks without crutches. On the fifth, they reach Jackson Lake below the Tetons. On the sixth, they cross the Divide into what is now Idaho, and so on, for days, all the way to Fort Hall, swimming rivers and walking through the sage desert. Ten miles from the fort, Russell's leg gives out, but they are spotted by friends and carried the rest of the way.

Lucky thing that Fort Hall was so close. With an arrow in your leg, and another in your hip, you wouldn't want to walk more than about 200 miles.

As a footnote, John Colter, the first of them all, quit the mountains after his narrow escape from the Blackfeet. "Too dangerous," he said. He went back to Missouri where he died, reportedly, of cholera.

92

Larry Ulrich

The Beartooth Plateau is a plateau on one side only. Seen from the south, as you drive out of Yellowstone toward the town of Red Lodge, Montana, the land rises gently through deep forest, into meadows dotted with lakes, then barren rock where you feel as if you're on top of the world. Suddenly everything drops precipitously thousands of feet to the Montana plains and the plateau becomes a stunning mountain escarpment.

94

Larry Ulrich

The Lamar Valley in northeast Yellowstone is the place mountain man Osborne Russell called the Hidden Valley, his favorite spot in the Rockies. He wanted to live out his life in this gentle valley surrounded by mountains that stirred his deep affection for geography.

Pat O'Hara

Russell wrote: "There is something in the wild romantic scenery of this valley which I cannot, nor will I, attempt to describe but the impressions made upon my mind while gazing from a high eminence on the surrounding landscape one evening as the sun was gently gliding behind the western mountain and casting its gigantic shadows across the vale were such as time can never efface from my memory."

96

Willard Clay

The Lower Falls of the Yellowstone stand at the head of the river's great canyon, a 1,200-foot-deep gorge of heat-altered rhyolite. The heat not only softened the rock, but changed its color as well. Yellowstone could have been named after this canyon in Wyoming, but it was not. There is another area of yellow rock far downstream in Montana. That Yellowstone has such a spectacular display of yellow rock is a fine coincidence.

Jeremy Schmidt

Jeremy Schmidt

The Yellowstone Plateau is a region of headwaters—of wild cascades and placid rivers filled with trout. The Firehole River flows through the world's greatest concentration of hot springs and geysers, while the Yellowstone River (*lower*) cuts broad curves through the superb wildlife habitat of Hayden Valley.

Pat O'Hara

98

The flow of hot, mineral-laden water is constantly changing course. Where the flow is strong, the terraces are brightly colored and growing. When the flow stops or goes in another direction, structures dry up, turn gray, and begin disintegrating. Eventually, the water will return with its powers of rejuvenation.

Algae color the white calcite, growing tiny forests on the bottoms of pools, floating in warm mini-islands on the water surface (*left*), or painting bright streaks where water temperatures are not too hot. Here, the lighter-colored streaks are made by algae surviving at the maximum temperature. As the water cools, green algae get a foothold.

Par O'Hara

100

Old Faithful takes on a different, more powerful character in winter. When the air is cold, the steam appears solid; the plume rises two or three times its summer height. If the temperature is really low, the geyser spray can fall as ice crystals—a miniature snowstorm made from boiling water.

Tom Till

A stand of lodgepole pine, killed by thermal runoff from springs near Castle Geyser, becomes rimed with frost during cold nights. Even during the day, icy mist hangs in the geyser basin, ebbing and flowing, creating an ever-changing fantasy world.

102

Tom & Pat Leeson

In 1872, Yellowstone was set aside primarily for its thermal features. Since then, it has become significant as a wildlife refuge. Grizzly bears are rarely seen and virtually never heard, but coyotes are a common sight hunting for mice in open meadows—three singing together in the distance can sound like a pack of ten. Pronghorn antelope, the fastest North American land animal, rely on speed and keen eyesight for protection from predators.

Tom & Pat Leeson

Tom & Pat Leeson

A mountain lion and her cub.

YELLOWSTONE IN WINTER

I lived in Yellowstone National Park for six years. When I left, I found that everywhere I went, I measured the distance back to Yellowstone. My internal compass had been forever magnetized. I was west, or north, or south of it. Something in my heart was always pointing back there. I never felt right until I moved back to where I live now, just south of the park.

One of my old Yellowstone friends had the same experience. He moved away and married a woman who had never been to the park. But the park was so much a part of him that she said, "It's like living with his old girlfriend." She wasn't sure she liked it. In the end, he too was drawn back to Yellowstone.

I didn't like the place when I first saw it. I was eighteen and on the loose for the first time in my life; I had my eyes on high mountains. The Tetons, the Winds, the Cascades—anywhere in the northern Rockies. Now those were mountains!

Yellowstone was too flat, I thought. There were a few unspectacular mountains on its perimeter but otherwise it was just a lot of trees and a lot of tourists. Nonetheless I saw the park a number of times, passing through on my way to more interesting places, always in a hurry. Yet, for some reason, I kept going back. I went one time in the fall during elk rut and came away feeling that something was happening in Yellowstone that made it special—not that I could identify what that something was. The next winter, 1973, I visited the park on skis, pulling a toboggan

for three weeks through the woods and over the frozen lakes. I saw bison covered with frost. I watched ravens and coyotes feed on winterkilled elk. I stood at night beside geysers exploding in sub-zero air. I could hardly believe my eyes.

Eight months later I was back at Old Faithful with a job. I had been hired as a winterkeeper; that is, I was expected to keep buildings from collapsing under the weight of the snow. I lived in a little house on the Firehole River behind Old Faithful Geyser. It was November. People were gone. The animals were moving down from the high country, and snow had begun to sift gently through the lodgepole pines.

Winter comes early to Yellowstone. It sneaks in on frosty feet one night in September and gently but firmly takes charge. For a few weeks, the two seasons spar with each other. Summer keeps a tenuous hold on the days; winter owns the nights. As the nights get longer, winter's influence grows. On cold autumn mornings, steaming rivers and geyser basins are lost in banks of fog that dissipate as the day warms, revealing delicately frosted vegetation. Soon the frost too has vanished. By noon, winter seems remote, but in fact it has just slipped away for a few hours.

By October, meadow grasses have all turned brown. Summer flowers, dry and rattling, have gone to seed. The sounds of insects disappear as they enter dormancy, or die of the cold. Night frost heaves the mud, adding a new pungency to the air. Water pipits, fresh from the Arctic, make a brief appearance before vanishing southward. Then one morning, after a night of rain in the valleys, snow flashes a warning signal from the mountains. It melts quickly in the strong autumn sun but up there on the mountaintops the shady places are very cold, sheltering small patches of snow. Winter has established a foothold.

For the park's animals, fall is a time of activity, for final fattening on the rich grasses and sedges of late summer, for the growth of winter fur, and for breeding. Bison are the first to begin breeding. Late in August the roaring of bulls echoes through the big open valleys. It's easy to mistake their roaring for bears, as if a convention of grizzlies were loudly contesting some issue or other. Then, in September, the elk begin bugling. Moonlit nights are filled with their strange, high-pitched, harmonic screams, sounds of power and urgency, wildly hormonal challenges to all within earshot. If any one sound evokes Yellowstone in the fall, this is it.

Some years the warm days last well into November. Each sunlit hour then becomes a thing of sharp beauty, a special gift that could be taken away at any moment. You appreciate these times knowing that when the snow comes in earnest (it never comes halfheartedly to Yellowstone), it won't disappear for nearly six months. Whether it comes in October or late November, that first snowfall is the signal for major animal movements. The migrating birds that have not yet gone south now depart for warmer climes. Bison, elk, deer, and bighorn sheep move down from the high summer range to the valley bottoms, along rivers and hot springs. Bears go to winter dens.

By December, snow lies deep across the entire park, filling the forests, blanketing the meadows. Days are short. The cold bites hard. The landscape is transformed into a glittering snowscape of exceptional beauty. Fog banks roll through thermal areas, stifling the view and muffling the already eerie sounds of boiling water and churning mud. Hundreds of hot springs and geysers continue to flow and erupt just as they do in summer but now, because the air is so much colder, their steam plumes rise two or three times higher. The mist, along with geyser spray, freezes on any available surface, forming strange and delicate ice structures. Entire stands of trees become covered with frost. They stand like marble statues of Druid monks.

Through this strange shifting landscape, frost-covered animals move in search of food. For them, winter is the season of testing. In one sense, spring and summer are nothing more than preparation for winter—or recovery from its demands. Animals that enter winter in good health are likely to survive. Those that do not will provide food for others—for the coyotes, foxes, bears, and ravens.

The power of winter is most evident on cold nights. I mean the really cold ones, when the temperature in late afternoon is already below zero and you know that by morning it will be 40 below, maybe colder. Yellowstone's official record stands at −66°F. On such evenings, sunsets come suddenly with no color except a premonitory tinge of violet just above the horizon. In the twilight, animals breathe heavy vapor that freezes to their fur. Bison stand in groups, as unmoving and enduring as rock outcrops. Elk lie in hollows at the edges of meadows. The night comes on, silent, cold, and brittle, settling over the land as if it has work to do.

Morning arrives fourteen hours later with a paling of the eastern sky, then a hint of rose in the gray. As the light increases, a far different world is revealed from the one last seen at twilight. All night, mist has risen from thermal waters, supercooled in contact with the air, and collected on all available surfaces— the trees, the buildings, the surface of the river, even the silent animals. Everything is deep in hoarfrost. Crystals might be a foot long and so delicate that the breath of an elk calf will shatter them. Bison have become walking fantasy creatures made of swaying ice. Their noses are black; their eyes peer from faces white with frost.

How do they survive? It looks hard and hopeless but they do. I remember a small herd of bison, about twenty animals, that spent most of one winter on a patch of thermally heated ground near Old Faithful. Not much grass grew there even in summer but it was their sole source of food for about five months. They worked that meager ground for all it would yield and then reworked it, swinging their massive heads, shoving aside snow that had already been shoved several times, probing with black, glistening noses . . . for what? What could they be finding to eat? I often skied through that meadow, or walked across it if there hadn't been any new snow for a week or two. Then the thermal

106

warmth would melt the meadow clear of snow and I could see its condition. By January, the ground looked barren, all vegetation cut down to its roots. Yet after snowstorms, with the meadow deeply buried, the bison would be out there swinging their heads, plowing their way down to those forlorn roots.

During storms they would move together as if seeking shelter or companionship. If the wind was blowing hard, the snow slanting viciously in from the west, they would sometimes move into the forest and lie down, their backs to the wind, and wait it out. It was a startling thing to come across them bedded down in the storm, all but invisible, covered with snow. If they saw me first, they would lurch to their feet and stand, swaying, snow falling off them in little avalanches. They were reluctant to move, and unwilling to lie back down while I was there. Whenever I saw them first (I soon learned to predict where they might be), I gave them a wide berth.

It was different during the really heavy snowstorms. Then there would be little wind, just snow falling silent and serious, pouring through the lodgepole pine needles with a crystalline hiss. In such storms, visibility was near zero. The snow might accumulate at rates of several inches an hour for days at a time. It was wet snow, near the freezing point, the flakes big and feathery for a time, then not flakes at all but tiny ice slivers. The middle of the day would be gloomy. Inside the house, I wanted the lights on. To compensate for the dampness in the air, I would turn the thermostat up five degrees. One storm, in March 1974, accumulated 7 feet of snow in ten days—7 feet even after compaction. Buildings were buried to their eaves. People dug tunnels to their doors and were more grateful than ever for shelter.

Of course there was nothing for the bison to do at times like that but endure. They would cluster together with heads down on one of several inactive geyser cones where the ground was warm enough to keep the snow from getting deep. They would stand together to wait out the storm. I would see them each morning; at nightfall, they would be there still, standing ever stolid, ever enduring, snow melting down their backs as fast as it piled up. They might stand there on that cone for three or four days, and never move enough for me to notice.

How did they do it? To a casual observer, the difficulties of survival appear nearly insurmountable. The occasional sick or dying animal, and of course the carcasses of those that have died, make the impression all that much stronger. When the temperature falls many degrees below zero (a common winter occurrence), it is hard to understand how any of the animals make it through the night.

Especially something like a chickadee, a tiny bird with an internal temperature of 105°F. Somehow it maintains that warmth on the coldest nights, 50 or 60 degrees below zero. The distance from its tiny heart (the size of a baby pea) to that deadly air is less than an inch, yet sitting on the branch of a pine tree all night long, this very significant little creature maintains a temperature gradient of 150 degrees or more. I used to go outside on nights like that just to feel the power of phenomenal cold. Wrapped in a huge down parka (4 inches thick, reaching to my knees) with insulated boots and pants, I could stay out for an hour or so of tramping through the geyser basin. I can't imagine sitting barefoot on a pine branch all night wearing a thin layer of feathers.

And what about elk feet? Obviously elk can't keep their feet as warm as their bodies, and they don't need to. There's no muscle to speak of in an elk's foot. It's mostly bone, cartilage, and tendon but it is alive. There's moisture inside. It has to move when the elk moves. How cold can a foot get? Think of how car tires sound on a cold day, and they're only rubber.

I wonder too about the perspective of elk calves. Born in the spring, raised and fattened on lush summer grasses, they know nothing of winter until they are surrounded by it. If they are capable of awareness (and why not?), that first winter must be a discouraging time for them. Suddenly the world changes and life gets really hard. They lack the comfort, unless it comes from instinct, of knowing that seasons are cyclic, that warmth follows cold, that grass will grow green again.

Of all the large animals, bison, with their thick fur and massive bodies, seem best equipped to deal with winter. Their humps, consisting of muscle and bone, serve as supports and motors for their snowplowing heads. Occasionally a lone bull will stay the winter in the high country, where he must push 4 to 6 feet of snow aside to reach feed. This is unusual, however; most bison retreat to areas of relatively shallow snow. There is evidence too that bison stomachs utilize what thin forage there is more efficiently than other animals.

107

Elk move snow with their hooves instead of their heads. They also feed in unfrozen rivers, standing in water up to their bellies, pulling up water plants. In late winter, when food supplies are gone, they might turn to pine needles, even though they cannot properly digest such feed. Elk have been found starved to death with bellies full of needles.

In Yellowstone's geyser basins, a few mule deer mingle with the elk, preferring shallow snow. Deer are browsers, eating not only grass but also twigs and the bud ends of shrubs.

Moose are also browsers. Their long legs make them the only big ungulates (hooved, herbivorous mammals, many of which are horned) to live in deep snow areas. They are able to survive on fir needles and willow twigs and to move through astonishingly deep snow. Yellowstone, however, has few moose; they prefer areas with lower elevations.

Surprisingly, coyotes have a harder time in early winter than later in the year. Snow covers the meadows and hides the rodents, which are an important source of food. Not until late winter will there be enough winterkilled carrion to feed coyotes, and then there will be more than enough.

I remember a bull bison that spent his winters behind my house. He was a loner, a common behavior for mature male bison. He walked into the meadow after the first big snow in November, fat from a long summer, his great shaggy mane in its prime, and there he stayed. The two of us watched winter pass through the meadow, he from his side, I from mine. By February, having grazed and regrazed the places where the snow was relatively shallow, he took to working the meadow margins. His huge head, 100 pounds heavy, plowed through the snow, piling it up on both sides of his trench. He pushed a wet and naked nose into the subzero pack, feeding on long-frozen, dry autumn grasses. As he pushed the trench forward, new snow and wind drift closed it up behind him. From my warm, well-stocked kitchen, it seemed that being a bison in the winter was a hard, losing business. But he had nowhere to go.

I was watching him through binoculars one time as he grazed away from me. All I could see were his strangely delicate hindquarters rising to the massive hump of shoulders and shag that hid his head. I tapped my binoculars sharply on the window several times. It was the inner window of two, and bison rarely respond to whistles, grunts, shouts, even car horns. But something in my knock, however slight, caused that great hairy head to swing to one side, ponderously, like an ancient iron-bound oak door, until one brown, frost-rimmed eye fixed on me as if through a knothole.

I doubt that he could see me. Bison eyesight is not acute, and he was 200 feet away. I stared for a long moment at that frozen half-face. Then it disappeared again behind those enormous shoulders. He began grazing again. Grazing and trenching as he was every morning in the gray dawn when I first looked out the window—as he was every evening when darkness stole my view of him. I was moved by the persistence of this animal, his grip on life, and by what seemed to be his sense of purpose, of dignity.

Each autumn I would look for him, hoping he had fed well during the summer. He never failed to appear. He was there when I moved from that house and, in my mind's eye, he still is.

Tom & Pat Leeson

A bison's fur is covered with frost. It looks cold, but the frost is a sign of the fur's insulating capacity. If the fur weren't so thick (about 6 inches on the hump), the bison would lose heat more quickly and the frost would melt.

110

W. Perry Conway

Winter is a time of testing for animals. When deep snow covers food sources, animals must conserve energy any way they can. Movement in search of food is an expensive activity. Above, mule deer follow in each other's tracks. Bison behave the same way; their trails form trenches between various feeding areas.

Tom & Pat Leeson

Jeremy Schmidt

Even in June, when bull elk antlers are growing beneath a skin of velvet, fresh snow can fall heavily enough to cover newly green grass. In the heart of winter, bison (*lower*) use their heads to plow deep snow from frozen grass.

112

Tom & Pat Leeson

The Yellowstone fires of 1988 were the biggest in human memory but not unusual over the region's long history. Large fires have burned at other times, perhaps more extensively. Above, three cow elk, dripping from a recent crossing of a river, stand in the eerie landscape of a burn.

Tom & Pat Leeson

Even in the center of a fire's destruction, some animals benefit. Predatory birds like this great gray owl feed well on abundant rodents and small mammals driven from the burned areas. Nature's cycles are profound and at times unfathomable.

Jeff Gnass

A stream pours through dense forest over large boulders, pausing reflectively in pools, collecting eventually in lakes like Idaho's Pend Oreille (*above*). Considering the overall dryness of the West, water, where it does gather, is a spectacular and precious thing.

115

116

Tom Till

Summer weather patterns in the mountains are very different from those of winter. During winter, storms roll in off the Pacific Ocean, riding strong jet streams and bringing the majority of the year's moisture. During summer, a barrier of high pressure builds over the Rockies. It takes a strong weather system to make it across the mountains in July.

Larry Ulrich

Tom Till

117

Most summer rain in the Rockies comes not from weather fronts but from thunderstorms that recycle moisture already in the ground. After a clear morning, clouds build over the mountains, gaining strength until, in the afternoon, there is lightning, hail, and heavy rain. By evening, the sky is again clear, but fresh moisture makes the night fragrant.

Tom & Pat Leeson

Montana is called Big Sky Country for good reason. Compared with Colorado, its valleys are wider, more spacious, easy on the eyes. Rivers flow broad and gentle through some of the best ranching country anywhere. Above, a rainbow appears after a summer storm.

Tom & Pat Leeson

In June, this Montana valley is as green and lush as Kentucky's bluegrass country. That will change quickly. By the end of July, any place not irrigated, like the hills in the background, will be bright yellow and crackling dry.

Raft on the Middle Fork of the Salmon River, Idaho.

Jeremy Schmidt

RIVER JOURNAL
MIDDLE FORK OF THE SALMON

Day One—July 16

I've heard good things about the Middle Fork of the Salmon: clear water, big rapids, great scenery, and lots of fish. It drops 104 miles through the wilderness of central Idaho from the Sawtooth Mountains to the Main Salmon River. Some call it the best wilderness run in the Rockies.

The river trip starts in Stanley, Idaho, a ramshackle little town whose main street is called the Ace of Diamonds. The name fits. Older buildings tilt like card houses. It looks as if a good wind could knock them over.

I meet Tom Tremaine in front of a Stanley motel. Tom is the head guide for Outdoor Adventures, an outfitter based in Point Reyes, California. There are fourteen of us on this trip—five guides, nine passengers. Boarding a bus, we rattle down the gravel road through rolling pine forest. This is rugged volcanic country, carved up by canyons, hard to travel in no matter how you go. Out of the bus window I catch glimpses of open blue space below spiked ridges: somewhere down there flows the river.

The rafts and the other guides are waiting for us at the junction of Boundary Creek and the Middle Fork, which at this point is a small, green, lively stream. Tom gives us a pep talk, tempering our enthusiasm for the river with practical warnings: "If you fall overboard and your foot gets caught under a rock, you'll drown. It's the only time a life jacket doesn't work. So keep your feet up." We nod soberly at this admonition.

The other guides are Dave, Earla, Mary, and Cathy. Dave is from Minneapolis, a commercial artist in winter, a guide by summer. Cathy and Mary are in training. They have both been running California rivers for Outdoor Adventures, but regulations demand that they run the Middle Fork three times before carrying passengers. So they row the baggage boat, and none of us are allowed to ride with them. Earla grew up in Idaho and guides most of the time for another river company. She's on loan this week—a guest appearance.

We have three rowing rafts and one paddle raft. Six of us join Dave in the paddle raft. With no baggage to carry, this is the sports car of the rafting world. You're in the action up to your elbows, sometimes over your head. When both hands are occupied with a paddle, it's possible to get tossed out.

Before setting off down the first rapid, we practice by paddling upstream, turning, crossing the river, spinning. Dave gives commands—"Left! Right! Forward!"

The oar boats go ahead. From above, the first rapid looks like a stone staircase with a little water flowing over it, the sort of thing you fall down not paddle through. In higher water, this would all be froth and turmoil. But this year has been dry. The drought of 1988 has been making news across the country. It hasn't rained in central Idaho for many weeks. There wasn't much snow last winter and nearly all of that has melted, even on the high peaks.

Measured by a gauge located halfway down the river, normal summer flows range around 3.0 to 4.0 feet. High water is 6.0 to 8.0. In 1974, Dave says, the river reached 14.0, too dangerous to paddle. Below 2.5 feet, boaters usually fly to Indian Creek, a backcountry airstrip 22 miles farther downstream. Tom expected higher water for this trip and decided two weeks ago to put in at Boundary Creek. Then the water fell to 2.2. It means bumping and scraping and getting out to push when rafts hang up on rocks. But no one complains. We all wanted to see the whole river.

"Ready or not!" shouts Dave as we enter the first rapid. "Left, left! Now right, pull hard!" Obviously, we are not yet a crack crew. Some pull left while the others go right, but we manage to avoid the one boulder that would give us real trouble. Otherwise, the raft pinballs harmlessly. Water splashes our faces, and we shoot into the pool below.

The river is incredibly clear. I see cutthroat trout against the rock bottom, 12 feet deep. Their furtive shapes glide over waving clumps of bright green algae and disappear into the blackness beneath boulders. A western tanager flies past, all yellow, red, and black. A merganser shepherds her brood ahead of us. She would fly if alone but her chicks (eleven of them) are flightless and she stays protectively with them.

A bigger rapid below. Dave puts on a serious face.

"There's blood on the rocks ahead," he says. "Rafts get pushed up against the cliff and people lose skin. It's awful." Dave, however, makes an unconvincing tough guy.

"Blood?" says one skeptic.

"No. Just lichen. Orange lichen. One of the simplest forms of life, if you don't count river guides."

We surge toward the cliff. Haystack waves wash over the raft. "Backpaddle!" shouts Dave. We dig in, riding a frothy pillow of water along the cliff's edge. It happens fast. Everyone gets soaked, and one paddler falls into the center of the raft, but no one loses any blood.

Approaching the next rapids, we notice a worried man waving a life jacket. "Pull over!" he shouts. Heading for shore, we see that a raft has capsized. Filled with water, it is plastered against a rock, held firmly in place by the current—"wrapped," in

river parlance. Wrapping can be dangerous, if you happen to get caught between the boat and the rock—an extremely rare occurrence, but a thought that keeps all river runners on their toes. In this case, the crew and passengers are lined up on the bank, hauling on a rope tied to a tree, trying to dislodge their craft. After much shouting and heaving, the raft swings free. But now it strains against the rope, threatening to tear the frame loose. A boatman leaps into the raft, slashes the rope with his knife and the boat, heavy with water, wallows down the rapids.

Thus warned, we take a cautious course well to the left of the threatening rock and pass without trouble. There are other good rapids, demanding careful maneuvering on our part. Velvet Falls, The Chutes, Sulphur Falls—each is different, each is a thrill. As we go, we get better at working together. The seven of us begin to feel like a team.

Then, just as the day is starting to feel long, and my back is tired from sitting upright on an inflated tube, we reach Elkhorn Bar, our first camp. Big trees shade the forest floor and the ground is springy underfoot. After helping to unload the rafts, I walk into the forest, up a gentle slope to a ridge. The river sounds fade, replaced by the sigh of wind in the pines. A hermit thrush sings its lovely, flutelike, ascending spiral. The river has brought us to the heart of a wilderness.

Day Two—July 17

In the morning, I wake to the sound of pots banging. I walk to the fire, where Cathy hands me a cup of hot coffee. The warmth of the cup feels good in my hands. Out in the river, I see a heron working the shallows. The bird stabs the water, comes up with something gleaming in its bill, and swallows it.

"Breakfast!" shouts Mary. The heron eats fish; we settle for scrambled eggs, sausage, fresh-baked muffins, slices of melon, and juice.

There's no hurry today. We spend the morning loafing around camp, adjusting to the scenes of the river, and getting to know each other. Our group includes two nurses, an industrial auctioneer, a certified public accountant, a truck driver, two securities advisors, a high school graduate, and me—a diverse and compatible bunch.

On the water again. The river picks up volume from feeder

streams, but still there's hardly enough to float the rafts. Getting through the rapids requires quick maneuvering—good practice for the bigger rapids to come. In some places, we jump out to haul the rafts over rocks. I enjoy standing in the beautiful clear water.

The canyon deepens. Above us, ridges climb ever higher, one above the other. Near Artillery Rapid, the forest suddenly thins to a few forlorn trees standing amid blackened trunks. In 1979, the Mortar Creek fire burned here, a powerful blaze that covered 65,000 acres before a heavy rainstorm put it out. Almost ten years later, new trees are about 2 feet high, growing amid the purple blush of fireweed blossoms.

Late in the afternoon, we run Pistol Creek rapids, a tight S-turn carved through a beautiful little canyon. The rapid ends in a deep pool of slowly turning green water. We make camp on a sand beach between the pool and the mouth of Pistol Creek.

I decide to walk up the creek on a pack trail toward a hot spring 3 miles away. We've arrived so easily that I have no sense of how deep in the wilds we are. Walking restores my perspective. According to the map, our camp is about 20 miles from the nearest roadhead, itself a long rough drive from a paved highway. No person has walked under these big trees for a while, but the trail sees plenty of traffic. I find prints of elk, deer, coyote, and cat—the big round tracks of a mountain lion. This place must really be wild if lions walk the trails.

The forest feels as dry as it should in late August. It is only mid-July, but already leaves are turning brown; raspberries and thimbleberries are bright red, and delicious. They slow me down. I pick my way through them, keeping in mind that bears are also fond of berries. I am leaning down low, peering into a brambly patch when I see the snake. Not all of it, just its midsection moving ominously past my hand. Tom warned us at the beginning of the trip: "Watch out for rattlesnakes." I freeze until the tail comes into view—no rattle, just the friendly taper of a gopher snake.

The hot springs are nothing but a dry whiff of sulphur on the banks of Pistol Creek. I turn around and head back to camp.

When I get there, Tom is frying blackened Cajun salmon. "I know it should be redfish to be authentic," he says, "but we *are* on the Middle Fork of the Salmon, after all."

Too bad the fish has to come out of plastic bags—it's frozen,

probably caught in Alaska. There aren't many salmon in the Salmon River these days. Too many dams on the Columbia; too much logging and habitat destruction on the spawning streams.

After dinner, we sprawl on the warm sand and tell river stories. Everyone feels relaxed. The air is warm. There are no mosquitoes. A great horned owl calls from the opposite bank. The big quiet pool turns slowly under the black, star-studded sky, and there's nowhere else any of us would rather be.

Day Three—July 18
The walls rise, and the river strengthens. The water forms a swiftly moving sheet, 1 or 2 feet deep, as clear as air. We float through rounded hills covered with brown grass and isolated ponderosa pines. It looks like central California.

I paddle an inflatable kayak in the afternoon. Good fun, good exercise, and lots of water in my face from the rapids. It feels strange to be happily soaking wet when all around rise the distant plumes of smoke from wildfires—constant reminders of how dry this place really is.

The smoke is thick in the sky over Loon Creek, where we're camping tonight. High enough that we can't even smell it, it colors the sunset a bright hot orange. The reason for choosing Loon Creek for a campsite, Tom says, is the hot spring complete with wooden tub located a quarter mile up the creek. It was built not by a hedonist, but by a prospector who used the hot water to thaw his placer claim in winter. He died when a dirt bank caved in on him. I wonder what he'd think if he could see fourteen laughing people up to their necks in the tub he built.

Day Four—July 19
In the morning, Tom confronts me with a plate of what he calls Norton eggs, scrambled with chunks of ham and vegetables. They taste fine, and even the name is okay until I learn about Norton. He was a woodsman whose face was mauled by a grizzly. The eggs, Tom says, resemble Norton's face—after the incident. That should not seem funny, but it does. On a trip like this, the humor goes downhill with the river.

The coffee is also a bit gruesome. Dave experiments, trying to settle the grounds with an egg. "It's Swedish coffee," he says. "I'm a Swede." He succeeds only in filling the brew with eggy flakes.

"What's the Swedish name for these things?" someone asks. "Mine are alive!" quips someone else. "And growing legs!" But it tastes good.

Down then over Tappan Falls, a sharp drop into a green bubbly pool and past Norton Creek, also named for the hapless, faceless man. We have lunch at Camas Creek between two smoke plumes from forest fires. The fires seem far away.

Again the landscape changes. High forested peaks come into view. Ridges run down from the forest across hot treeless hills to end in sharp shadowed cliffs at the river. There is plenty of water now. The rapids are bigger and more challenging and nearly continuous. The Middle Fork keeps us busy.

Late in the day we pull over at Rattlesnake Cave, an overhang with a sandy beach and a screen of brush. On an overhanging wall there are pictographs—red human figures, some shooting arrows at a deer. One figure has feathered wings for arms. There is also a battle scene, weathered and hard to see. These haunting and lovely drawings were made by Sheepeater Indians, a branch of Shoshone. They lived in small bands throughout the Salmon River country, hunting and fishing and keeping a low profile even among other Indians. Then, in the 1870s, when they objected to the influx of gold miners, they were rounded up in an action called the Sheepeater War and exiled to a reservation in southern Idaho.

That night we camp at Survey Creek among tall pines. There is a ruined cabin down the shore and three pioneer graves, two of which hold unknown men. I walk up the hill behind camp and find tracks of mountain sheep and elk on a grassy flat. The river, visible in both directions, provides a tough travel route through incredibly rugged country. No one knows how many untold stories and unmarked graves lie in the secrecy of these hidden canyons.

Day Five—July 20

From the middle of the river on Tom Tremaine's boat, I watch a golden eagle fold its wings against the blue sky and streak like a missile into a bush high above the river. Chukars, birds like large quail, explode from the bush, fleeing for their lives—successfully, it appears. When the eagle emerges and takes to the air, its talons are empty.

Downstream a few miles, Waterfall Creek tumbles to the river through a great pile of house-sized boulders. "I'll show you a special place," says Tom. We climb steep slabs of rotten stone to a grotto. The creek pours over the rim above our heads, filling the grotto with windy mist. This water has come down 5,000 feet from a cluster of granite pinnacles called the Bighorn Crags. We can't see them from the river, but we feel their snowmelt on our faces.

Day Six—July 21

Our last day. I wish we were back at the head of the Middle Fork. I'm just now getting attuned to life on the river, to its fluid rhythms, to the continuous sounds of water working on rock. I find myself staring hard at the canyon, trying to take it all in. The walls are very high now and smoothed by glaciers. I can barely distinguish the large trees growing on the tops of the soaring granite pinnacles. This morning is particularly beautiful for an odd reason. Smoke from the forest fires fills the canyons like a thin mist, softening edges, creating a sense of mystery and depth.

Then we are into a series of big rapids: Rubber, Hancock, Devil's Tooth, House Rocks, and others. The waves are high enough to swamp the paddle raft. The rocks challenge the maneuvering skills we've practiced for five days. We do well, despite the big haystack wave at Hancock Rapid that throws two of us into the river. There's no danger, bobbing along behind the raft. In fact, being so intimately involved with the river is a thrill. I'd like to come back when the water is high, to feel the adrenaline of the really big waves.

Around noon, the Middle Fork carries us into the Main Salmon River. It comes almost as a rude awakening to realize that our trip is nearly over. I've come to love this idyllic blue-and-white river, tumbling through its canyon like a living gem from a time when the earth was pure. I want to keep going. Down the river, across Idaho, into the wilderness. Who knows where?

Larry Ulrich

S unrise light bathes cottonwood trees along the Henrys Fork River in Island Park, Idaho. This gentle landscape within the Rockies is the result of a great volcanic explosion earlier than, but similar to, the one that devastated the heart of Yellowstone some 600,000 years ago. In both cases, whatever mountains may have existed before the eruptions were simply blown sky-high.

126

Tom & Pat Leeson

The West owes much of its diversity to the uneven (some would say unfair) distribution of water. Summers are dry; winters are wet. The west side of a range gets plenty of water, while the east side is a desert. Above, cattle stand belly-deep in well-watered Montana grass after a morning rainstorm.

David Stoecklein

While summer thunderstorms pound the southern Rockies with moisture from the Gulf of California, southern Idaho enjoys good weather for rattlesnakes. There are deserts in the Rockies where raising horses and cattle requires 40 acres or more per head.

128

David Stoecklein

The Bannock tribe of Shoshones is famous for its horses and horsemanship. Sacajawea, the Indian woman who accompanied Lewis and Clark, was Shoshone, and it was her tribe that provided the American expedition with horses and directions to the Columbia River.

129

David Stoecklein

Each summer, more than 100 powwows, festive gatherings of Native Americans, are held throughout North America. They provide a chance to show off traditional dress, music, dancing, and equestrian skills—and to celebrate native pride.

A combination of performance, competition, and county fair, powwows are happy events to which all are invited.

David Stoecklein

130

The Mountain West required resourcefulness and independence of settlers, who responded with personal strength and determination to match. Although many viewed the West as a place to make a quick buck and get out of, others, particularly ranchers, came to stay. Today, family ranchers feel as strongly about their land as the Indians who once called the same places home.

David Stoecklein

Ranching never has been an easy way to make a living. Even with the help of electricity and modern machines, the raising of cattle requires long hours and hard labor in whatever weather happens to prevail. But try to tell a rancher that he or she would be better off taking a town job with regular hours and you'd get laughed out of the room.

David Stoecklein

David Stoecklein

133

In 1936, Ketchum, Idaho was a railhead and center for sheep ranching. During winter, it slept. Then came Sun Valley, the first of the Rocky Mountain ski resorts, attracting movie stars and celebrities from all over the world. Snow, it turned out, could be more valuable than wool. The country around Elkhorn (*above*), a resort development adjacent to Sun Valley, shows why the area was considered such a perfect setting.

St. Mary Lake on the east side of Glacier National Park, Montana.

PART THREE
GLACIERS & GRIZZLIES

Red Rock Falls, Glacier National Park, Montana.

Pat O'Hara

THE NORTHERN ROCKIES

The mouth of the Columbia River was first discovered in May 1792 by the American sea captain Robert Gray. Five months later, a subordinate of Britain's Captain George Vancouver entered the Columbia estuary and sailed about a hundred miles inland to plant the British flag. Both countries declared an interest in the Pacific Northwest but neither made any move to solidify its claim. After all, the mouth of this unknown river was a long distance from Philadelphia, then the capital of the United States. It was even farther from England. Ships had to make the arduous passage around the tip of South America. And for what? No one knew where the Columbia came from or what sort of country it drained.

Nonetheless it seemed reasonable to expect that such a large river (big enough for British ships, after all) might provide an easy water route from the Continental Divide to the Pacific. The United States became interested after acquiring the Louisiana Territory, which included the entire Missouri River drainage.

For that reason, among others, President Thomas Jefferson sent Lewis and Clark on their famous expedition. Jefferson hoped to clear up the geographical and political confusion and open the way for American trade from coast to coast. It was a grand dream but as the American explorers learned, the country was far grander. Although boats might navigate most of the Missouri River, canyons on the western slope were impassible even for horses.

Or were they? Perhaps, thought the directors of Canada's North West Company (a fur-trading outfit in competition with the Hudson's Bay Company), perhaps a feasible route lay farther north. Accordingly, in 1810, David Thompson was commissioned to find the northern headwaters of the Columbia and to trace the river to the sea.

The Canadians already knew something about the Rockies. Since 1799, the North West Company had maintained a trading post called Rocky Mountain House in the foothills north of modern Calgary. They knew that the mountains stretched a long distance north and south, and they assumed that the Columbia began on the other side of the range but that was as far as their knowledge went. Nor did the Blackfeet Indians, with whom they traded, offer any help. The Blackfeet understood the relationship between modern weapons and power. For some time, they had been lording it over other tribes in the area, and the last thing they wanted was for the likes of David Thompson to cross the Divide and set up trade with their old enemies, the Kutenais.

For their part, the Kutenais had been clamoring for trade. David Thompson himself had made a brief contact with them in 1800. A few years later he had actually camped beside the Columbia River but he had failed to recognize it because it flowed north at that point. In 1810 he knew better, and this time he made it all the way to the ocean.

The Columbia never developed as a trade route. The War of 1812 interfered. The Blackfeet interfered. Kutenai country produced few beaver pelts. The topography was too rough. The market in beaver fell apart. And in 1846 the forty-ninth parallel became the international boundary, giving the lower Columbia to the United States. Even today, the Trans-Canada Highway takes a twisting, tortuous path across the Rockies to the coast. Simply put, there never was an easy way.

In any event, the settlement boom in the Canadian mountains began from the west coast, not the plains, as a result of gold discoveries in the Fraser River Valley. The mineral-poor Rockies received little attention while all eyes were on the goldfields. And why not? Legend has it that one man in the Cariboo Valley washed 96 ounces of gold from a single pan.

Attitudes were bound to change, of course, once the gold was gone and people began to appreciate mountains for something other than the metal they might contain. In 1885 the first railroad was completed across Canada. It traversed the Rockies through the modern townsites of Banff and Lake Louise. Within two years, a thriving tourist industry was launched and Canada's first national park was established (called Rocky Mountain National Park, it was eventually enlarged and renamed Banff).

Like David Thompson, most travelers today catch their first glimpse of the northern Rockies from the east, on the plains of Alberta or Montana, at a distance of a hundred miles or more. Expansive wheat fields roll along mile after treeless mile. Highways stretch as straight as a surveyor's compass line under a limitless blue sky. Then, gradually, the land begins to swell. It lifts in a series of low ridges like immense waves, and from the top of a wave comes the first view of the mountains, snow-topped and gleaming—a great shining wall.

That wall stretches virtually unbroken for about a thousand miles. It begins north of Helena, Montana, where the mountains collect themselves to make a single unified gesture. To the south, at the latitude of northern Wyoming, the Rockies lie scattered across some six hundred miles, three states, and dozens of subranges. There's no such clutter in the north. Near the Canadian border the Rockies narrow to about a hundred miles; at Lake Louise, in Banff National Park, they are scarcely fifty miles wide.

This narrowing, far from diminishing the range, lends the mountains an aura of strength. Almost all of the Rockies from this point north have been deemed spectacular and wild enough for preservation. Starting in Montana, the Scapegoat, Bob Marshall, and Great Bear wilderness areas take up roughly 1.5 million acres of prime alpine country. Where they leave off, Glacier National Park presents its superb collection of striated giants—big colorful mountains, sharp pinnacles, deep valleys, more than two hundred lakes and about fifty glaciers. Its slopes are strewn with wildflowers and a huge variety of plants. On the wet west side, shady trails lead through coastal-type forest of red cedar and Douglas fir. On the east side facing the plains, drier conditions support dense stands of aspen reminiscent of central Colorado.

Glacier National Park roughly marks the southern edge of the great continental glaciers that enveloped the landscape during the Ice Age. Other, smaller ice sheets occurred as far south as New Mexico, covering the high peaks but not the lower valleys. It was only in the north, where everything was under thousands of feet of ice, that valley glaciers were able to perform their magnificent sculpting.

The result is a landscape dominated by mountains with nearly vertical, smooth sides, the outlying ridges and buttresses sheared off, alluvial debris scooped up and carried away by grinding ice. Glaciers did the carving and then cleaned up, leaving in their wake a monumental topography. Something about that soaring curved shape lends northern mountains an aura of massive strength not found in mountains to the south, where valleys are ruggedly contorted and many peaks stand hidden behind subsidiary ridges. You can best observe this larger-than-life aspect of northern mountains from viewpoints partway up those grand slopes; for example, from Glacier's Going-to-the-Sun Highway. Or, for that matter, from numerous hiking trails.

Fifty miles north of the border begins the great complex of Canadian preserves including four national parks (Banff, Jasper, Yoho, and Kootenay), several wilderness areas, and numerous provincial parks such as Top of the World, Elk Lakes, Mount Assiniboine, and Mount Robson. Robson at 12,972 feet is the highest peak in the Canadian Rockies. Assiniboine (11,870 feet) is one of the most perfect. Together they display the elements that make the Canadian Rockies famous: mountains that are not

138

just big but enormous, spangled with snow and ice, subject often to violent weather, and spectacular to look at.

Most of all, they are big. Maybe too big. The Canadian Rockies are built on a scale that is difficult to comprehend. Entering Banff for the first time, you get a sense of how Chinese provincials must have felt when first seeing the Forbidden City, home of their God-Emperor. The place was too big and rich for mere humans. You gaze across immense valleys at the feet of sweeping mountain walls, and you don't know where to begin. You see it all through these parks, stunned motionless by the scenery. Gosh, you mean a person can hike here? It seems you'd walk all day and get nowhere.

Well, it isn't that big. The most famous beauty spots are welcoming enough to the eye and to the casual walker: Banff's Lake Louise, Yoho's Lake O'Hara, Jasper's Angel Glacier.

From Jasper National Park, the Rockies continue north through the Willmore Wilderness Park into roadless country, the home of wolf, wolverine, grizzly, caribou, and eagle. Hundreds of miles north, the mountains gather themselves for one final scenic effort in the area of Kwadacha Wilderness Park before fading away to foothills along the Liard River.

In all that great length, the eastern plains beat against the mountains like the sea upon a precipitous shoreline. The mountains begin where the plains end, as simple as that. You're either in the Rockies or out of them and there is no confusion about which is which. On the west side, however, things are a bit more complicated. This becomes obvious if you drive through the Rockies on the Trans-Canada Highway. Sure enough, the highway emerges from the mountains at Golden, British Columbia, but what are those other ones ahead? They look as big as the Rockies and at least as impressive. They have snow and glaciers and lakes and forest and wildlife and all the other things you expect of mountains, including two national parks—Revelstoke and Glacier. But they aren't the Rockies; they are called the Columbia Mountains.

In Colorado, subranges of the Rockies crowd shoulder to shoulder halfway across the state. They all have different names, but they are all part of the Rockies. The difference in Canada is that the Columbia Mountains are almost 100 million years older than the upstart Rockies. Back before the Laramide Orogeny

stirred things up and long before the Rockies rose beside them, the Columbia Mountains overlooked the prairies, or rather the shallow sea that covered the middle part of North America at that time.

The Columbia Mountains include four subranges called the Cariboos, the Monashees, the Purcells, and the Selkirks. They are all made of old, hard, metamorphosed rock, in contrast to the sedimentary masses of the neighboring Rockies. Because they are nearer to the coast, the Columbias are wetter than the Rockies, pulling down great quantities of snow in the winter (33 feet is the annual average at Rogers Pass), supporting about one hundred glaciers and growing lush forests. These mountains are famous among skiers who love powder snow and can afford the steep price of hiring helicopters. They are also famous among rock climbers for places like Bugaboo Spires, where clean granite pinnacles soar toothlike above the glaciers.

If you continued from Golden into the Columbias, you would cross them at Rogers Pass in the superb heart of Canada's Glacier National Park. A bit farther down the highway is Mount Revelstoke National Park, where you can follow a road from fragrant interior rain forest (cedars, ferns, and giant skunk cabbage) all the way to alpine tundra. Beyond Revelstoke, the driving gets interesting as highways wriggle their way through the tangled geography of southern British Columbia. An easier way south is to return to Golden and follow a broad valley called the Rocky Mountain Trench. Caused by a geologic fault that runs along the western slope of the true Rockies all the way from their northern beginnings into Montana, this feature represents the physical separation of the Rockies from the Columbias. Along this line the Rockies rose, forming an escarpment almost as striking as their eastern front.

Where the Columbia Mountains sink into obscurity just south of the U.S. border, the Cabinet Mountains lift their heads, elbowing in against the northern salient of the Bitterroots. All around them, on both the Idaho and Montana sides of the line, smaller mountains fail to rise above a dense cover of well-watered forest. Living among the shadows in mature stands of subalpine spruce and fir are a great variety of wildlife including a tiny population of woodland caribou, relatives of the famous barren ground caribou that live in the Arctic. They feed in winter on lichen

139

called Old Man's Beard that hangs in long strands from tree branches, but only where the climate is damp and only in mature forest.

In light of the forest fires that swept the Yellowstone Plateau in 1988, it is worthwhile to recall the far-greater fires that devastated northern Idaho in August 1910. Fire crews had been busy all summer. By August 15, more than 3,000 fires had been controlled, but many more still burned. Thousands of firefighters were scattered throughout the mountains when the fateful day arrived.

August 20 brought high winds and dry air. Fires from the Salmon River to the Canadian border (a total of 1,736 fires) roared to life. Lolo National Forest Supervisor Elers Koch wrote in a report thirty-two years later:

The sky turned a ghastly yellow, and at four o'clock it was black dark ahead of the advancing flames. One observer said the air felt electric, as though the whole world was ready to go up on spontaneous combustion. The heat of the fire and the great masses of flaming gas created great whirlwinds which mowed down swaths of trees in advance of the flames.

In two days, fires leaped 30 to 50 miles, sending fire crews scrambling for their lives. A third of Wallace, Idaho went up in flames as evacuation trains steamed for safety. Four small towns were entirely destroyed. Over 3 million acres burned and at least eighty-five people died, seventy-eight of them firefighters.

Finally, one more range warrants mention: the Mission Mountains that form an impressive rampart above Flathead Valley. The Missions are known for their rugged, deep-cut topography. The level-floored valley is known for having been once—or rather, many times—filled with water. Modern Flathead Lake is a small pond compared to historic Missoula Lake, whose old water lines can still be seen, like bathtub rings, on the slopes of the Missions. It happened during the Ice Age, when glaciers moving south from Canada blocked the Clark Fork River. The resulting lake was 2,000 feet deep. Periodically, the ice retreated or the water cut a channel, and the lake drained with devastating results. It happened several times. In the space of two or three days the entire body of water, enough to fill half of Lake Michigan, roared westward at speeds as high as 45 miles per hour. It was not a river. It was an eruption that hurled 9.5 cubic miles of water per hour across what is today a peaceful landscape.

That wasn't very long ago, even in human terms. The last ice advance may have occurred as recently as 5000 B.C., making it quite possible that people witnessed one of Missoula Lake's astounding floods. Compared to then, we live in quiet times.

140

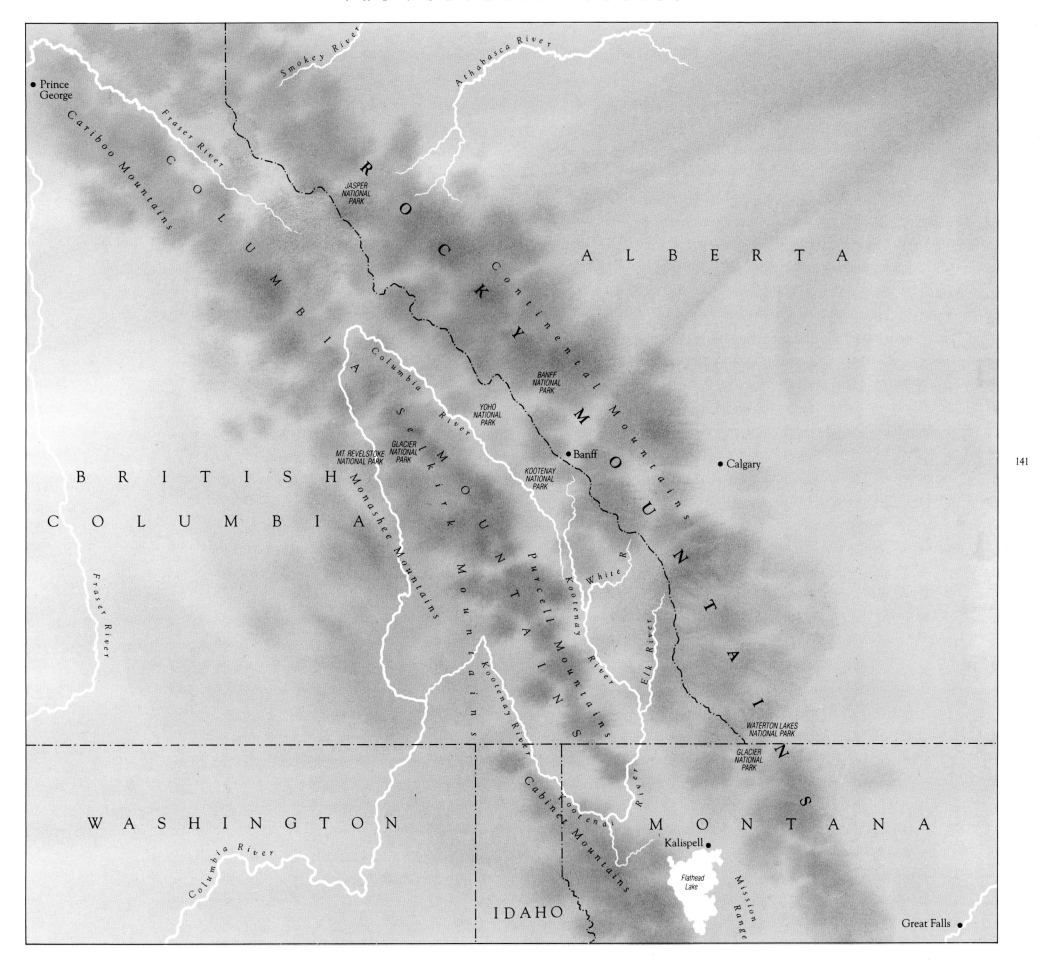

Prince
George

Smokey River

Athabasca River

Cariboo Mountains

Fraser River

ROCKY

ALBERTA

JASPER
NATIONAL
PARK

C O L U M B I A

Continental Mountains

Columbia River

BANFF
NATIONAL
PARK

YOHO
NATIONAL
PARK

M O U N T A I N S

Banff

Calgary

141

B R I T I S H

MT. REVELSTOKE
NATIONAL PARK

GLACIER
NATIONAL
PARK

KOOTENAY
NATIONAL
PARK

C O L U M B I A

Selkirk Mountains

Monashee Mountains

White R.

Purcell Mountains

Kootenay River

Elk River

Fraser River

WATERTON LAKES
NATIONAL PARK

Kootenay River

GLACIER
NATIONAL
PARK

W A S H I N G T O N

Cabinet Mountains

M O N T A N A

Columbia River

Kootenai River

IDAHO

Kalispell

Flathead
Lake

Mission Range

Great Falls

142

Larry Ulrich

Lewis monkeyflowers and arnica, Indian paintbrush and asters join in the lush but short-lived display on Glacier National Park's Logan Pass, just one of many superb alpine meadows accessible by highway throughout the Rockies.

Tom & Pat Leeson

Chief Mountain, on the east side of Glacier National Park (Montana), is a geologic anomaly. The rock beneath the mountain is younger than the mountain itself, the result of what is called the Lewis Overthrust. As the northern Rockies tilted upward, a large chunk of rock, like a sheet of ice in a pressure ridge, broke loose and slid downhill on top of younger rock.

144

Tom & Pat Leeson

The Prince of Wales Hotel stands at the north end of Waterton Lake, a 12-mile-long lake that crosses the international boundary between Glacier National Park in Montana and Waterton Lakes National Park in Alberta, Canada. At the other end is a remote place called Goat Haunt, where trails lead in several directions into wilderness valleys.

Tom & Pat Leeson

Bison graze in Waterton Lakes National Park beneath massive, layered mountains typical of the northern Rockies. Loose sedimentary cliffs and wide glacial valleys like that of Waterton Lakes (*opposite*) are characteristic of the region.

Tom & Pat Leeson

The Rockwall, rising above Floe Lake, is representative of the Kootenay National Park back country in British Columbia. Cliffs like these, apparently inaccessible, are commonly used by mountain goats (*above*) as safe havens from predators that lack their extraordinary climbing skills.

150

Pat O'Hara

The wild grandeur of the Rockies can be too much to comprehend, their scale intimidating. The quiet places like this boat house on Emerald Lake in Yoho National Park seem filled with peace. A gentle glide at sunrise can provide a perfect counterpoint to a walk among the high wind-torn summits.

Pat O'Hara

The simple green world of a marsh is a deceptively complex place. Shallow waters teem with frogs, water snakes, muskrats, a huge variety of insects, and wading birds. You need to look closely to see them.

Grizzly bear, northern Rockies.

THE COMPANY OF WILD ANIMALS

In the southern Rockies, you think a lot about spirits. The land is full of them—in the ancient pueblo towns, in silent Anasazi cliff dwellings, in the old Spanish mission churches. Some spirits you can see, like the Zuni Shalako dancers and the Hopi kachinas. You see them and, even if you consider them to be nothing more than costumed humans, you can't help thinking about the spirits they represent. They are the spirits of the land and its culture. They can change the way you feel about your surroundings. They enrich the experience of being there.

Sadly, some of the spirits are gone from the southern Rockies. Aldo Leopold, the conservationist, wrote about the disappearance of one such spirit. It lived on a mountain in New Mexico called Escudilla, a distinctive landmark visible for miles around. The spirit was that of a solitary grizzly bear.

No one ever saw the old bear, but in the muddy springs about the base of the cliffs you saw his incredible tracks. Seeing them made the most hard-bitten cowboys aware of bear. Wherever they rode they saw the mountain, and when they saw the mountain they thought of bear. Campfire conversation ran to beef, bailes *and bear.*

Then the government sent a trapper whose job was to kill predators. He had a hard time hunting that bear. It took him a month, but he managed to kill it—the last grizzly in that region.

In death, the lord of the mountain was just a carcass. Not even the pelt was worth saving. Only after the grizzly had been killed did Leopold, who worked for the Forest Service at the time, and the other rangers begin to consider the loss. Recalling the conquistador Coronado, Leopold wrote:

We spoke harshly of the Spaniards who, in their zeal for gold and converts, had needlessly extinguished the native Indians. It did not occur to us that we, too, were the captains of an invasion too sure of its own righteousness.

He continued:

Escudilla still hangs on the horizon, but when you see it you no longer think of bear. It's only a mountain now.

Today you have to go north to find grizzlies, into the wilderness areas of the northern Rockies. The Yellowstone region supports an island population of two or three hundred grizzlies. Otherwise, they live only to the north of central Montana.

In the northern Rockies, forests seem deeper than in the south. Distances feel longer. The land resonates with a sense of wildness. A series of parks and roadless areas, joined together along the spine of the mountains, protects a vast, nearly unbroken tract of wild land. The national parks include Glacier, Waterton, Banff, Yoho, and Kootenay; augmenting them are provincial parks like Assiniboine, Mount Robson, and Kananaskis, and designated wilderness areas including Great Bear, Bob Marshall, and Mission Mountains. In a distance of some 800 miles, only four highways cross the Continental Divide. Nearly all the mountain country in that stretch is protected in one way or another.

Fortunately, so are a variety of wildlife that have disappeared or become scarce farther south—not just the grizzly but also the wolf, the bald eagle, the trumpeter swan, the bighorn sheep, the mountain goat, the cougar, and the wolverine. Where these animals live, the spirit of wildness lives. Like canaries in an underground mine, their survival reassures us that the land in which they—and we—live is still healthy. Even if we never see them, knowledge of their presence changes the way we feel about a place, as the old bear affected the way Leopold felt about Escudilla. The land, especially where the likes of grizzlies are concerned, seems to hold, somehow, more possibility.

Possibility? Of what, being eaten?

As a matter of fact, yes. In grizzly country, humans are not the toughest animals around. There's something stronger out there, a secretive animal that we don't know enough about, that can take us apart as easily as a cat dismembers a chipmunk. Grizzlies do just that—very rarely, but convincingly when they do. They are one of the last big animals on the continent capable of hunting us down and having us for dinner. It's a good thing that they don't want to, that instead, they expend great effort in avoiding contact with humans.

Even so, the presence of that unpredictable, potentially dangerous power is always close to a hiker's thoughts. What a difference it makes to my sleep, lying in my tent on a silent moonless night and hearing a footfall out there, to think it could be a bear.

About ten years ago, a bear in Montana (I never saw it, so I don't know if it was a grizzly or a black bear) inadvertently taught me a lesson. I was on a backpack trip. I had bushwhacked most of the day, crossing high ridges, following game trails heavy with the tracks of elk and deer. It was autumn. The elk were in rut. Their strong bull-smell permeated the air. I could hear them bugling deep in the forest.

That evening, I camped on the edge of a large, wet meadow. I lit a fire, and when it was hot, I emptied a small package of pork sausage into a frying pan. It smelled good. I sat back against my pack and let the sausage sizzle. It smelled really good. I was tired and getting hungry. I sat in the fading light, daydreaming.

Suddenly, a bear shouted in surprise. I don't know how else to describe the sound. It was a shout, loud and guttural and sudden. It came from the edge of the forest just yards from where I sat looking at the sky. The shout was followed by a crashing sound running back into the woods and then silence. The bear, I guessed, had followed the wonderful smell of pork sausage until, just yards from me, it saw (or smelled) the scary truth.

No more daydreams. I quickly ate the sausage, built up the fire, burned the fat, and scorched the pan dry. I scrubbed my hands and face in the river and vowed to never fry meat in the backcountry again.

That night, there was a full moon. A herd of elk came out into the meadow. I could hear them moving through the grass. The cows were calling their strange querulous mewing calls. Then they were running, stomping heavily, very excited. And I thought, he's out there, out in the meadow, spooking the elk. It was a long time before I slept.

Another time, walking through lodgepole forest, I practically stood on an elk calf hiding under a log. I had been watching nervously for bear. I'd seen tracks close by. Then, as I stepped over the log, this furry shape erupted at my feet. It stopped my heart, and it occurred to me that only in bear country could a wobbly elk calf be such a scary thing to see.

Bighorn sheep are not a bit scary. But, like grizzlies, we know far too little about them. Reputed to be the wariest and most noble of game animals, sheep are thought to be shy of man in the way eagles are, or condors—forever wild to the very core of their nature, not to be tamed, and conquered only by the very best of hunters.

Tom McBride, of Helena, Montana, laughs when he hears such talk. He should know. During the early seventies, the Idaho Fish and Game Department needed someone to make a winter survey of sheep in what is now the Frank Church River of No Return Wilderness. They hired McBride. They gave him a 60-

154

power telescope and told him that even with that, he would have trouble getting close enough to do meaningful observation.

McBride did better. After about two weeks, he was sitting, he says, "within a stone's throw of half the legal rams in the area." He hadn't gone there to hunt them, and as if they recognized that fact, they had accepted his presence. He followed them around all winter. He rarely bothered with the telescope. Does this mean their reclusive reputation is unwarranted?

McBride says no. "Sure they run from hunters. You would too, if someone came sneaking up at you with a gun. That doesn't mean it's some kind of natural, instinctive reaction to man—that's just the way sheep are. You go in armed with a little humility instead of a gun, and you find an entirely different animal.

"Sheep have learned how to recognize a predator, and to escape one when it comes. That's an important survival skill. But it should make us wonder. I mean, how is it that they can tell the difference between a man who wants to kill them and one who doesn't? Isn't that worth some thought?"

McBride told me about "his" sheep one winter night in Helena. I asked him if he could show me. He said he'd love to. We went the next spring, he and I and two friends named Mark and Jean, just after the winter snow had melted off south-facing slopes. We hiked up from the road and camped in the valley bottom.

"That's where they'll be," Tom said, pointing to a grassy area at the base of vertical cliffs. "They spent last winter there. It's a good place. They don't worry about anything coming down from above, and they can keep their eye on whatever moves below."

That meant us, among other potential threats. Without trying to hide, we wandered slowly through the valley bottom. "You can't sneak up on them," said Tom. "Their eyesight is eight times as sharp as ours. Good as eagles."

I asked what they would do if I somehow managed to approach without their knowing I was there? How would they react on seeing me?

"They'd be gone in a moment," said Tom, "and you wouldn't see them again, I guarantee it. The trick here is to be accepted by them so they don't run just because you come close."

So we let the sheep look us over for a few hours. Tom instructed me on the art of approach. He said, "Be humble, body and mind. Man is an aggressive animal. Curb the aggression. And don't care! If you really want to get near them, you never will. They pick up on that somehow. The harder you chase the less chance you have."

Don't care? That was hard for me. I tried to take my mind off the band of sheep by looking at things close to the ground. I discovered ticks, hundreds of them, clinging to the shrubbery and grass stems. Sometimes there were three or four on a single stem, balanced on its outermost tip like tiny acrobats, front legs spread out wide, waiting for a warm-blooded target to come by. I moved a hand near one. It waved its legs. I supposed alarms were sounding in its tiny nervous system: "This is it! This is it!"

If grizzlies were one-tenth as fierce as ticks, bears would rule the world. The moment I touched its legs, the tick had me. It moved as if spring-loaded, launching itself toward the climax of its life. To do or die, to get blood and lay eggs and produce offspring. Of all the ticks in the world, few even make contact with a host. This one was more successful than most. I pulled it off and crushed it.

From then on, I had less trouble keeping my mind off the sheep. There were lots of ticks. We kept our pants tucked into our socks and checked each other's scalps regularly. While we sat eating lunch, Mark noticed two ewes emerge from a willow thicket 500 feet below us. They were climbing toward the other sheep and would have to come past where we sat.

"Good," said Tom. "We'll just go along with them, sort of 'See who brought us.' Meantime, don't even look at them."

We pretended not to notice the ewes. They came within 100 feet of us, their hooves making delicate sounds on the scree. Then we followed, meandering, talking only a little, keeping our elbows in and our heads down—as if grazing. Pretty soon, we were close to the band. A ram stood up, looking nervous, but then sat back down. We did too.

All afternoon, we stayed about a hundred yards from the sheep as they foraged along the mountain slope. Occasionally, the rams would challenge each other, smashing horns in the classic bighorn battle. Just practicing, Tom called it. They would get serious during the rut in late fall. This looked plenty serious to me. Once I saw a piece of horn fly loose after a collision.

The sun set, the temperature dropped, and we left.

155

"Thanks Tom, that was wonderful," I said.

"Just wait till tomorrow."

"What, there's more?"

"You'll see."

The next day we repeated our slow meandering approach, but spent less time sitting. By noon we had reached a grassy knob.

"They're moving this way," said Tom. "Let's just stay here and see if they come to us."

And it happened! In a half hour, the four of us were suddenly surrounded by three mature rams and about fifteen younger males, ewes, and lambs. Their eyes were beautiful—liquid brown pupils with black, vertical irises. Their muzzles were soft, black, and velvety. They paid little attention to us, as we had hoped. We were just there, part of the meadow. Some lay down. The three rams butted playfully at each other. Their horns made a hollow sound like heavy wooden mallets.

I felt gifted by the presence of these animals. I sat very still, afraid to break the fragile mood.

But it wasn't as fragile as I imagined. After a time, Mark went higher to slide down a snowfield on a small sheet of plastic. A crowd of ewes watched him come down, snow flying, and then rushed over as if curious to see what on earth that was, moving so fast. Mark stood up to an inquisitive crowd of sheep lining the edge of the snowfield, cocking their heads and staring.

But the most amazing thing happened to Jean. She was sitting on a rock when one of the rams came up behind her and, lowering his head, pushed against her back with his heavy horns. Just a nudge, very gentle. He could have knocked her flying.

"What's he doing?" I asked Tom.

"I don't know. I've seen rams do that to women before. Never to men."

The ram repeated the nudge, then went back to tapping horns with the other rams. Gradually the band moved off the grassy knoll. We went down the mountain to our camp and dinner.

In the past century, many of the important animals of the Rockies have faced hard times, victims of the frontier attitude that nature's bounty was unlimited. Some species nearly vanished; the buffalo is a prime example. Others disappeared from much of their natural range and survive today only in isolated sanctuaries. For many, their future existence hangs in the balance.

Sheep, elk, and other game animals have enjoyed an ironic advantage over predators like the wolf: Because hunters value them, they have been protected from extinction—even reintroduced to areas where they had disappeared as a result of overhunting, habitat loss, and other factors. The elk herds of New Mexico and Arizona, for example, are descendants of elk trapped in and moved from Wyoming.

Predators, on the other hand, have never been seen as desirable sport animals—and certainly not as a source of meat. On the contrary, wolves, mountain lions, coyotes, bears, and others were thought to compete with humans for food, be it wild game or domestic cattle and sheep. They were considered bad animals, to be destroyed not protected. Bounties were placed on their heads and just about everyone, even wildlife professionals, approved.

Things are different now. Careful research has shown that habitat and food supply—not predation—is the major factor in limiting wildlife populations. The attitude now is that all species are important in some way, and that any extinction is an irretrievable loss. We've learned to appreciate the role predators play in keeping their prey species healthy; and perhaps more important, we've learned to see them as beautiful creatures that add enormously to the richness of our natural world.

Not all the news is bad for threatened animals. The coyote has astonishing reproductive abilities; it has survived all efforts to exterminate it and has actually extended its range. Mountain lions, still hunted, are nonetheless widespread throughout the Rockies although they are rarely seen. Bald eagles, osprey, and other birds of prey have increased their numbers since protective measures went into effect in the past three decades. Trumpeter swans, once on the brink of extinction, are making a comeback. So, it is hoped, are whooping cranes. Grizzlies, now that so few survive south of Canada, have become a national treasure. And there is serious talk of reintroducing Rocky Mountain wolves in Yellowstone National Park.

It is a pleasant thought, for me, to be in Yellowstone some cold autumn evening and hear, the way they sounded a hundred years ago, a chorus of wolves mingled with the bugling of elk.

Tom & Pat Leeson

A mixed band of bighorn sheep graze on winter range in Jasper National Park, Alberta, Canada. When summer comes, the animals will disperse to feeding grounds in the high country. The rams will form small bands of a few animals separate from the ewes and lambs.

Jim Brandenburg

158

Jim Brandenburg

The timber wolf, also called gray wolf, once occupied most of the Northern Hemisphere, including the entire Rocky Mountain region. Not limited to forested areas, wolves were often seen following bison herds on the Great Plains, until the herds themselves disappeared. Wolves have retreated steadily northward in the face of expanding agriculture until today they are found in the Rockies only to the north of central Montana.

Jim Brandenburg

Wolves were once regarded as completely undesirable varmints. They were shot, trapped, and poisoned to extinction even in wildlife refuges like Yellowstone National Park. But attitudes have changed over the years. Wolves are valued now for their role in maintaining the balance of natural ecosystems and for the aesthetic pleasure of knowing that wolves are still part of the wilderness world. Plans are now being made for their reintroduction in some areas.

160

Larry Ulrich

Trails, as beautiful to walk as they are, reveal the fragility of alpine soil—no more than a thin mat several inches deep. Damaged tundra can take 400 to 1,000 years to recover, pointing out the importance of walking lightly in the high country.

161

Larry Ulrich

Opabin Creek flows into a pond below Mount Huber in the Lake O'Hara region of Yoho National Park. The turquoise color of the pond water is caused by fine glacial silt in suspension.

Tom & Pat Leeson

I n Canada, the Rockies increase in scale
until they seem too big for mere humans.
You stand and look at them the way you
gaze at the moon or at Mars—too big and
too remote to touch. It's all a trick of the
eye. The mountains are indeed big, but not
that big. A few hours spent walking will
reveal many treasures, perhaps a glimpse of
a bull elk, handsome in his autumn finery.

163

Pat O'Hara

Mount Assiniboine, reflected in the waters of Sunburst Lake, is a classic example of a glacial horn—a mountain sharpened by glaciers working from all sides, undermining the cliffs that, becoming steeper with time, appear almost vertical.

Pat O'Hara

Great mountains are made of little stones. The pebbles on the bottom of Bow Lake in Banff National Park (Alberta, Canada) have fallen from the cliffs of surrounding mountains. Because the sedimentary material of the Canadian Rockies is relatively soft, rocks are continually falling and sliding downhill, preventing vegetation from growing on loose slopes.

Cotton grass and Pedicularis (elephant's head), Banff National Park, Alberta, Canada.

ALPINE ROADS

Anyone who thinks that the tops of mountains should be left to mountaineers and other rugged types has never driven Going-to-the-Sun Highway in Glacier National Park.

Nor, for that matter, any of the other Rocky Mountain roads that climb to rarified altitudes. It's almost like riding a ski lift, going up these roads. They are all spectacular. They offer wonderful views and a chance to experience at close range the arctic world of snowfields and alpine tundra. In Colorado the Evans Peak Road, west of Denver, ascends to 14,264 feet, the highest point reachable by auto in North America. Nearby Pikes Peak is almost as high; people have driven the road to its summit since the 1880s when the trip by horse carriage took more than five hours. In Rocky Mountain National Park, the Trail Ridge Road follows an old Indian trail across the Continental Divide at nearly 12,000 feet. And between Aspen and Buena Vista, the unpaved but stunning Highway 82 crosses Independence Pass at 12,095 feet. The amazing thing about this last road is seeing, high on the most difficult of surrounding peaks, the trails and diggings of now-abandoned mining efforts. They provide a measure of the energy men can summon at the hint of gold.

In Montana, on the northeast corner of Yellowstone National Park, the Beartooth Highway provides an interesting geology lesson. Heading north, the road climbs gradually on an uptilted block of granite past dozens of sparkling alpine lakes and gentle meadows. Then, abruptly, the earth drops away, and you are gazing down a great escarpment, almost as if you had driven up the gradual west side of the Teton Range and come suddenly to a view of Jackson Hole.

For sheer scenic expanse, no alpine road surpasses the Banff-Jasper Parkway. It runs for 142 miles through a stunning intermontane valley past lakes and waterfalls and the great blue faces of glaciers, reaching a scenic climax at Sunwapta Pass and the famous Columbia Icefield.

There are other alpine roads throughout the Rockies, less known, little used, and often rugged enough to require a four-wheel-drive vehicle. But if you had a chance to see only one of them, you couldn't do better than the Going-to-the-Sun Highway. It traverses the very heart of Glacier National Park, a place considered by many to contain the finest expression of Rocky Mountain scenery. At no other point in the Rockies are the mountains more gracefully formed or more stately. Lakes shimmer in the summer sun, wildflower meadows can take your breath away, and wildlife appears at every turn.

Starting from the east, the road skirts the shores of St. Mary Lake, a long sinuous body of water beneath peaks with alluring names like Red Eagle, Little Chief, Mahtotopa, Siyeh, and, as you might expect, Going-to-the-Sun. After leaving the lake, the road cuts through deep forest for a few miles, climbing all the while, until it emerges on the face of a near-vertical cliff. At this point, you begin to sense what a dramatic and unusual highway this is. But take it slowly; there is much to see, whether you do nothing more than stop at a pullout and glass the cliffs for mountain goats, or walk off the road into lush wildflower meadows dominated by the white spikes of beargrass or the intense reds of Indian paintbrush. All along the road, alpine streams plunge from sparkling snowfields. Waterfalls are numerous. At one point the road is soaked by a cascade thundering down the cliff.

It's easy to see, as you approach Logan Pass, how the park got its name. The signs of glaciers, their footprints so to speak, are everywhere. Today, nearly fifty glaciers adorn the park, beautiful to look at but miniatures compared to their prodigious ancestors. Several ice ages have left their mark on the Rockies, forming great ice caps thousands of feet thick, enveloping all but the highest mountain summits. The most recent episode was the Wisconsin Ice Age, which lasted from about 70,000 years ago until 10,000 years ago. Recent evidence indicates that the small glaciers we see today are not remnants of the ancient ice. Apparently they are relative newcomers about three centuries old—miniature, perhaps shrinking, models occupying the grand landscape carved by their epic ancestors.

If you could watch a glacier through a time-lapse film covering thousands of years, it would appear to be a living creature, hungrily gnawing into the mountain, tearing loose the native rock, creating dramatic and distinctive landscapes. In the process, valleys are broadened, changed from V-shapes to U-shapes. Ridges are honed to knife edges. Pinnacles are sharpened. When several glaciers chisel different sides of a mountain, they transform it into a matterhorn. If one glacier carves faster than its tributary glacier, the result, once the ice has melted, is a hanging valley.

All this takes time of course. If the glaciers on either side had had a few more thousand years to work, Logan Pass might have been reduced to an arête instead of the generous saddle-shape it is today. In fact, if you look up from Logan Pass at the Garden Wall, you are looking at a classic glacially sharpened ridge, an arête many miles long.

Examining a map of Glacier Park, you'll notice that all the big lakes—MacDonald, St. Mary, Sherburne, and the others—are long and narrow. They occupy glacially scoured valleys. Each is held in place by glacial deposits, moraines, dumped long ago at the mouths of the glaciers. The same is true of the smaller cirque lakes that dot the park. One of the nicest of these is Hidden Lake, a short walk through alpine meadows from the parking area at Logan Pass. You walk through carpets of wildflowers to an overlook, and there it is far below, tight against the sheer cliffs, pure, dark, and sparkling.

This assumes, of course, that the day is clear—not at all something to be taken for granted. The one thing about a mountain pass that no one can ignore is the change in climate. An alpine road takes you not only up into the mountains, but into the weather as well, and the change from valley bottom to mountaintop can be dramatic. Too often, a high road is the last place you would want to be.

As a rule of thumb, air temperatures drop three to five degrees for each 1,000 feet of elevation gain. That explains the classic summer view of snowcapped mountains standing above warm, sometimes sweltering, valleys. You could start up Going-to-the-Sun Highway with your air conditioner running and switch to your heater by the time you reached the pass.

Changes in plant life tell the story. From the deep forest surrounding St. Mary Lake, you ascend through smaller and more twisted trees into a region of frozen tundra, dwarfed shrubs, and herbs. If the road went high enough (this one does not but it comes near), you would eventually reach the zone of perpetual ice and snow, where the average temperature stays below freezing and conditions are similar to those in polar regions. You might find lichens growing that high but even those find life difficult.

Because they span such a range of climates, mountains serve as telltales in the landscape's rigging. If you know the elevation of various peaks and ridges, you can see how low the clouds are. The behavior of clouds indicates how cold the air is at different elevations or how hard the wind is blowing; sometimes a clear snowline shows where the temperature falls below freezing. You can tell time by watching mountain shadows. You can clock the seasons through changes in foliage; while summer is yet green and vibrant on the valley floor, a flash of golden aspens high on a ridge

170

warns that cold weather has already arrived up there.

Late in the summer, there's a good chance of thunderstorms on the high passes, although for some reason, the most severe of these occur not on places like Logan Pass, but in the Front Range of the Colorado Rockies. A storm in 1984 threw hail the size of grapefruit at Denver.

For most of the year, places like Logan Pass are scenes of extreme weather. The wind howls, deforming trees and building snowdrifts that last well into the summer. When weather is on the move, mountain passes develop life-threatening conditions. Not only is the cold intense, but the winds are literally staggering—especially in winter, when weather patterns are strongly from the west.

The record snowfall for the Rockies is held by Wolf Creek Pass in southern Colorado: 837 inches in the winter of 1978 and 1979. The official record low temperature for the United States outside of Alaska—minus 69.9°F—occurred at Rogers Pass in Montana (not to be confused with Rogers Pass in British Columbia, a place notorious in its own right for an astounding rate of snowfall).

With conditions like that, it's no wonder that trees and wildflowers growing at altitude are stunted. No wonder it takes hundreds of years for alpine meadows to recover from the damage of human foot traffic.

On the other hand, there are times when mountaintops are more pleasant than valleys. It happens in winter, between storms when the sky is clear and the air calm—in other words, during spells of high pressure. Then come inversions. At night, with no cloud cover to serve as insulation, heat radiates into black space. The mercury plummets. The air, becoming more dense as it chills, flows like water off the mountains to pool in valley bottoms. Because this pool of air is so cold and heavy, and because the snow-covered ground stays frigid when the sun is shining, the bitter air just sits there, immovable, collecting smoke from woodstoves, sometimes developing a fog of supercooled droplets, and making life miserable until a weather disturbance breaks the stagnation.

If you stayed in the valley on days like that, you might think it was a bitter gray day. But get up a few hundred feet and suddenly you emerge into what skiers like to call a "bluebird" day—

the sparkling perfection of winter. The air gets warmer, not colder. It isn't at all unusual, during an inversion, to hear on the morning ski report that the base temperature is something like minus 10 degrees, while on the summit, it's 25 degrees and sunny.

Mountain weather is variable and hard to predict. It can be dry, wet, cold, warm, windy, and calm all in a few hours' time. One day in Browning, Montana, the temperature dropped 100 degrees. Almost anywhere in the high Rockies, a minus-30-degree night can easily be followed by a 35-degree day. Or consider what happened in the Black Hills city of Spearfish in January 1943: In the space of two minutes, the temperature went from minus 4 to plus 45 degrees!

There's a saying in New England that if you don't like the weather, wait a minute. Obviously, the saying holds just as true in the Rockies but people here add that if you still don't like it, just move until you find what you want. If you go up in elevation, you (usually) find cooler air, except during inversions. You can also choose between the wet side or the dry side of a mountain; the shady side or the sunny side; the windy side or the sheltered side.

The differences can be dramatic. Suppose you've driven across Montana in the summertime, when temperatures can be over 100 degrees and wheat fields in late July are already golden and looking ready for harvest. You get to Glacier Park and start up the Going-to-the-Sun Highway through groves of shimmering green-and-silver aspen trees, past tumbling brooks, into shady, fragrant conifer forest, and finally above timberline, where wildflowers cover the slopes. You could be excused for thinking you had arrived in a wet climate.

But you would not be prepared for the west side of Logan Pass. Suddenly the mountains that seemed well endowed with greenery become incredibly lush. The place drips with plant life and water. On the valley floor, instead of aspen trees, venerable cedars are rising through luxuriant banks of ferns.

Throughout the Rockies, the west side of any range is often the wetter side because clouds are forced to unload moisture on windward slopes.

Are there no patterns? Yes, but only in the most general terms. Most years, the Rockies see relatively wet winters and dry summers. In winter, strong jet streams flow more or less straight in from the Pacific. During summer, warm temperatures combine

171

with the height of the mountains to create a barrier so that very little rain falls.

Whatever moisture does make it to the Rockies always comes from the west, from the Pacific Ocean. You never hear of a snowstorm passing over New York headed for Colorado. But the situation is more complicated than that. Some of the biggest storms to hit the Rockies are called "Easters" because they seem to roll in from the east, across the high plains; and they occur most often in spring, around Easter. That is the season when large weather systems, rotating counterclockwise, lift moisture from the warm Gulf of Mexico and spin it around into the front ranges of the Rockies. These storm systems proceed east across the continent, but the winds on their northern edges blow toward the west, so that if you stand in the foothills, the entire storm seems to be coming from the east. The results can be spectacular. One April day, 7 feet of snow fell northwest of Denver during one of those storms.

The range of conditions is something westerners learn to accept, to cope with, and eventually to be fond of. As long as their houses aren't located in a wind tunnel.

Speaking of wind, you would expect it to be strong on mountain summits. The atmosphere is a blanket of air about 6 miles thick. As it moves inland from the Pacific Ocean and encounters the mountains, the bottom 2 miles or so of that blanket—the densest layer of air—must squeeze upward to get past. In doing so, it speeds up and creates high winds on high ridges.

What might come as a surprise, however, is that the lee sides of mountains, not the windward, suffer the strongest winds. It's a bit like being at the bottom of a waterfall. The air, having gotten past the constriction of the mountains, comes howling down the eastern slopes. Boulder, Colorado is one of the country's windiest places, blasted by winds as high as 140 miles per hour. The basin just west of Laramie, Wyoming, on the east side of the Medicine Bow Mountains, is another famous wind zone. And in the northern Rockies, the people who live on the east side of Glacier Park suffer continually from wind. I once met a man who lived near Browning, Montana in a house that had no windows on its west-facing wall. It was a noticeable feature of the house, because he could have enjoyed a spectacular view of the mountains. The problem was that each year heavy winds blew out his west-facing windows, so he finally gave in and boarded them up.

There's a little town called Babb near the eastern end of the Going-to-the-Sun Highway. It boasts a gas station, a bar, and not much else. As the local story goes, the wind blows so hard so much of the time that guys come out of the bar a little tipsy and get knocked flat on their faces. You can tell who's been out drinking, they say, by who's wearing the bandages. Then one day the same guys come out of the bar, having learned by now to lean upwind, and fall flat on their faces again. Why? Because the wind suddenly quit.

Is that a true story? Perhaps not. But it shows how westerners love their weather, and the mountains that shape it.

172

Mountains and mountain weather are inseparable. Weather shapes the mountains, bringing rain and snow, creating glaciers, determining what plants and animals survive in what places, breaking apart rocks and carrying them away. In turn, mountains shape the weather, collecting clouds, causing updrafts that build thunderstorms, and determining where rain and snow will fall. These clouds and this sunset would not be here without the mountains to catch them.

Moonset at dawn, Banff National Park, Alberta, Canada.

Pat O'Hara

POWDER

We stand, three of us, high on a mountain ridge in British Columbia. Beneath us, a magnificent sweep of untracked powder snow. Fifty miles of the Rockies are visible to the north and south, dwarfing us and the tenuous line we have traced from the trees 2,000 feet below. Our tracks, barely visible on the brilliant snow, emerge from timberline, skirt a line of cornices on the ridge and then climb the crest itself to the high point where we now stand. It took two hours to make the climb, yet we can be back in the trees in five minutes.

"Who's first?" says Pat. No one moves. We are torn between two desires: to ski the powder, ski it now, ski it forever, and yet we are reluctant to leave this high place. The sun is bright and warm. There is no wind. As strong as the pull of the powder may be, we feel no hurry. For this is the physical high point of the day. We left camp five hours ago with just this place in mind.

So we stand, riveted. Rapture of the heights.

At last, Art Twomey, my old friend and mountain guide, pushes off. In a moment he is a hundred feet down the slope, churning up a billowing contrail. I whoop and follow. At first my skis are parallel, gaining speed, floating higher in the soft snow, headed straight down. When I have enough speed I begin turning, crossing Art's track, matching his rhythm, going right where he went left in a rhythmic series of eights. The snow banks over my shoulders at each turn, then I am floating high and gaining speed for the next. Ankle-deep, then in to my waist, buried in soft white, weightless snow. We soar and dip through snow as light as air—settled cumulus—and with the blue sky all around and the day so clean and cold, it comes close to flying.

Powder snow is a phenomenon largely indigenous to the Rocky Mountains and the smaller ranges grouped around them. More air than solid, the best powder has a water content as low as 3 or 4 percent. That means that 100 inches of snow will melt down to 3 or 4 inches of water and 97 inches of nothing. Mountain ranges famous for the quality of their powder include the San Juans, the Wasatch, the Tetons, the Bridgers, the Purcells, and the Cariboos—all of them in or near the Rockies and none of them on the Pacific coast.

The interior ranges get this dry, low-density treasure because storms coming off the Pacific drop most of their moisture on the first mountains they reach. The coastal ranges act as wringers, hauling down immense loads of wet, heavy snow. People talk none too fondly of Sierra cement or Cascade concrete. Sometimes skiers in Washington have to wear raincoats to stay dry.

In the Rockies, the terms for snow are different: angel dust, cold smoke, white gold, the steep and deep. They all refer chauvinistically to the driest, lightest snow on the continent, and perhaps in the world: God's Own Finest Rocky Mountain Powder.

Some people are willing to go to great effort for powder, even trekking deep into roadless country, where there are no ski lifts and you never cross another skier's track. The wilderness in winter is beautiful and the skiing unbeatable, but you pay a price.

As an example, consider a trip I made in Canada's Yukon—not the Rockies, but conditions were the same. I was again with Pat Morrow. Our plan was to ski around Mt. Logan, Canada's highest peak. We had expected the trip to be hard, but things were getting out of hand. The weather had been terrible. We had over a hundred miles of skiing ahead of us, yet for five days of trudging over the gloomy glacier, we'd seen nothing of the mountains. It had been snowing the whole time.

Each day followed a dreary routine: Guzzle a fast breakfast, load up the ice-encrusted gear, and then ski like madmen for an hour to get warm. We navigated by compass, guessing our position relative to the obscured mountains and the avalanches we could hear thundering down off them. We took lunch on the move—frozen cheese, frozen chunks of meat, chocolate that could crack a tooth. It was too cold to sit down.

Below us, we knew, were crevasses. We tied ourselves together with a rope, on the theory that if one fell through, the other would anchor him and give him a chance to climb out. It was a nasty thought, spinning in the blue ice void between a slit of sky and black death below.

At one point, as the swirling storm darkened, I was following Pat's ski trail. I didn't know he had stopped until I got close enough to see him, about 50 feet ahead. He waved urgently at me to stop.

"Crevasse!" he shouted. Pushing slowly uphill through deep snow, blind as Oedipus, he had felt a ski tip hit air and had halted with inches to spare. We went back a shaky 50 yards and camped for the night.

Even that was no pleasure. The nights were long and our sleeping bags got damper by the day. Inside mine were chunks of frozen body moisture the size of walnuts.

"What are we doing here?" I said. "Why not Mexico, why not come here in the summer?"

Pat grinned a silly grin. "Too many mosquitoes in the summer," he said. As good a reason as any.

When I mention wilderness skiing to people who haven't done it, they often wonder what the fun is. I suppose their question is a mild equivalent of the hackneyed Everest query that George Mallory tried so long to answer. It is said that his famous reply—"Because it's there!"—was tossed off in a moment of irritation. For his questioners, those three words provided a convenient handle on what they regarded to be either his genius or his insanity. For Mallory, it got them off his back. He had grown weary of trying to explain the unexplainable, to give an answer that any mountaineer knows to be intuitive and not rational. Wilderness skiing, like mountaineering, provides its own justification. One learns it by doing it. To ask why is like asking a person newly in love why he loves. Try as he might, his answers will make no sense to anyone who thought it was a reasonable question to ask. He might as well say, "Because it's fun."

Fun is perhaps the one thing wilderness skiing is not. It can be awfully hard work. Snow gets heavy and difficult to move through. Weather can be impossible; the temperature takes wild fluctuations, raining one day and freezing hard the next. Ice gets into all your gear. The tent that fit so nicely into its stuff sack at home refuses to conform, and your hands go numb trying to make it do so. Large amounts of fuel are needed to melt snow for drinking water. In the morning your hot cereal freezes on the spoon. Tea, by the time it's brewed, is a lukewarm soup with noodles from last night's dinner floating like scum on the surface.

One of the main pleasures of summer hiking is the time spent in leisure—watching a sunset, sitting beside a tumbling stream, or just resting in the warm grass. In winter, comfort is stripped away. Days are short but chores take longer. You have to keep moving to stay functional. You have to carry piles of extra gear—more clothing, more food, a bigger sleeping bag, mittens, hats, overboots, emergency supplies, snow shovels, goggles, and, of course, skis and poles.

No wonder it can seem pointless at times. But the pleasures of winter in the mountains are as intense as the miseries. Life takes on a sharp, unforgiving clarity, demanding precision in all you do. In storm or under blue skies, at dawn or in the middle of a moonless night, in dense forest or high on a snow-fluted peak, winter can be exquisite in its crystalline perfection and appalling in its scale. The combination of the terrible and the beautiful can result in moments of incendiary beauty, moments that transcend any summer experience, any moment grown out of ease and leisure.

One winter, on a full-moon night, I skied 7 miles to a backcountry cabin. The cabin stood on the shore of a large lake, above which rose a single massive mountain. Two friends had gone ahead and I followed their tracks through shadowy forest. It was rolling country with gentle hills, broad valleys, and small streams.

The skiing was easy, the night calm and not very cold. Owls drifted through the upper branches of the pines. Snowshoe hares disappeared like little ghosts into the shadows as I glided by. Once I rounded a corner and nearly ran into a moose in a small clearing. I was going downhill fairly fast and all I saw was a sudden large flailing motion beside me, then I was past him.

I wonder what he thought of that encounter.

When I slipped into the big silent valley leading to the lake, the mountain rose up on my right, looming whitely. It was completely covered with snow, brilliant against the black sky. Here the surface had been packed by the wind. The terrain was slightly downhill, the skiing effortless. The only thing moving, I drifted like a snowflake for 2 miles to the beach, clattered over a pressure ridge and out onto the flat surface of the lake.

From there it was a short half mile to the cove and the cabin. Already I could smell wood smoke. Then, rounding a piney point, I saw the warm light of kerosene lanterns glowing behind small windows across blue snow. It looked cozy and inviting, but even so, I remained outside an extra ten minutes in the silent moonlight, reluctant to break its spell.

Among the less-idyllic experiences was the time a bull bison tried to kill me. I thought at the time he meant murder. In retrospect, I can't be sure of his intent, but I still feel lucky to have escaped injury. I had skied up one side of a small hill, pulling a toboggan, as he trudged up the other. We met at the top, mutually surprised, 50 yards apart.

I stopped. He did not. I moved to one side. He changed course to intercept me. I struggled out of my toboggan harness. By the time I was free he had accelerated into a ponderous run, all four hooves hitting the snow at once, his head low. I'd seen bison run like that only one other time, when two bulls attacked each other like freight trains. Whoever thought up the name for a bulldozer had bison in mind.

With skis to my advantage, I cut straight back down the hill through deep snow. The bison followed, trampling my toboggan as he came, but the snow bogged him down. He stood over my gear for two hours as I skied back and forth in the valley below waiting for him to give up and move on.

Cantankerous bison aside, the most dangerous things in the winter backcountry are avalanches. The forces involved are enormous, the speeds can be terrifying, and the effect devastating. Of course the same can be said of trains, speeding bullets, and drunk drivers. The trick is to avoid them, like the other hazards of cold weather: hypothermia, frostbite, thin ice, snow blindness, and so forth.

Nasty things. Among skiers, the worst experience is the source of continual morbid discussion. But when it comes to the biggest thrill, whether in the backcountry or at a developed ski resort, there is total agreement. Everyone who knows it loves deep powder.

Once you learn to ski powder, you're spoiled forever. No other skiing quite matches up. Hard pack gets boring. Ice is intolerable. Moguls (the bumps formed in a slope by the passing of many skiers), at one time fun to negotiate, now become simply obstacles. Powder skiers stay home unless there is fresh snow; they live from one storm to the next.

Kept too long from powder, the true addict gets to quivering in the knees when he thinks about it. His stomach turns and his eyes gleam. The only cure is to don the ratty old wind pants and the pack that should have fallen apart years ago, and go skiing.

I have a friend like that—over thirty, married a time or two, still living most of the year in his van, teaching skiing when he needs money. He hobnobs with ski area executives and skis with some of the wealthiest people in the country, yet he owns no more than he can carry into your spare room in three armloads. Except for skis, that is. Scattered in the basements and garages of friends all over the Rockies are at least thirty pairs of his skis. He maintains that deep powder skiing is the best physical sensation known to man. Or woman.

He may be right. I have occasionally skied powder that ran over my head without slowing me noticeably. I've skied off cornices and dropped through the air so hard that I disappeared under the surface, popping out 30 feet lower with my face covered in snow, whooping and giggling like a kid at Christmas. When it's that good, you can't think of anything better.

It's not always good. It's not always God's Own Finest in the Rockies any more than it's always cement in the Sierra. Two years ago, I got to talking with a friend about powder. It was autumn and we were both eager for skiing.

"The really perfect days, when you get both sun and deep powder, I could count on one hand," he said.

"Come on, it happens more often than that!"

"No, it doesn't. You get a lot of pretty good days, but the best days, the great days, those are rare times. You remember them like landmarks."

Indeed. I kept track that winter. It was a mild winter with less than normal snowfall, but there was plenty of good skiing from the second week of November until late April. I skied every chance I had. I watched the weather with a keen eye. In that whole winter, I never did have a perfect day. By spring, I got to wondering if I'd only imagined perfection.

Certainly the horrible conditions are not imaginary, although you might wish they were. Skiers have a whole separate vocabulary for bad snow. The sun can turn powder to mashed potatoes, which is about as descriptive a term as boilerplate. You can't ski boilerplate, you negotiate it. Boilerplate is a hockey rink set on edge. Then there's breakable crust, a sort of intermittent boilerplate upon which you accelerate to frightening speed before falling through into a bed of sharp-edged ice splinters.

In the spring you hit patches of mud that stop you as surely as brick walls. Crud, a catchall term for any snow that's been partially melted, refrozen, or stirred by the wind, feels like the contents of the town dump. And sugar snow refers to granular, unconsolidated crystals that roll like ball bearings. Skis dive into

it like panicked submarines, all the way to the rocks.

Also in spring, the increasingly strong sun melts the top layer of powder, so you sink through slush to cold snow below, which freezes the whole mess and globs up 6 inches thick. In my experience, only fresh bison droppings are more frustrating. (And not only to skiers. In Yellowstone National Park I saw a speeding snowmobile hit a frozen bison chip, lying like a rock in the road. The machine tipped right over. Luckily, the driver was well padded.)

I once crossed a meadow covered with snow but underlain by slightly warm water from a hot spring. Dense, springy grass held the snow up over the water, but it did not support me. I found myself standing in powder above my knees with my feet buried in soft oozy mud. This, I thought, is lousy skiing. But I said something more colorful than that.

Times like those you might as well go home and hit your head with hammers for fun, or take dives off the roof into a pile of scrap metal. You mentally list enemies to whom you could donate your skis. The worst is when your thoughts drift sacrilegiously to places where no one has ever seen a ski, where the only cold thing is an ice cube melting in a rum cocktail. Maybe Honolulu, or Mazatlán.

But then comes another day when the cumulus settles on the peaks. You climb high onto a gleaming ridge and push off into space. You rise and fall with the rhythm of your turns like an albatross on broad ocean swells. This is powder, God's Own, head-deep, ultralight. You feel as pure and shiny as the mountains themselves.

On days like that, up there in the rafters of the world, you don't even stop to pity the poor slobs in Mazatlán.

188

Bibliography

Berry, Don. *A Majority of Scoundrels*. Ballantine Books, New York, 1961.

Chittenden, Hiram M. *The American Fur Trade of the Far West*. 3 vols. Francis P. Harper, New York, 1902.

Chronic, Halka. *Roadside Geology of Colorado*. Mountain Press Publishing Company, Missoula, Montana, 1983.

_____. *Pages of Stone*. The Mountaineers, Seattle, 1984.

Conley, Cort. *The Middle Fork and the Sheepeater War*. Backeddy Books, Cambridge, Idaho, 1977.

_____. *Idaho for the Curious*. Backeddy Books, Cambridge, Idaho, 1982.

DeVoto, Bernard. *The Journals of Lewis and Clark*. Houghton Mifflin Company, Boston, 1959.

Feder, Harlan, ed. *Colorado Winterguide*. Wayfinder Press, Ouray, Colorado, 1984.

Herrero, Stephen. *Bear Attacks: Their Causes and Avoidance*. Nick Lyons Books, New York, 1985.

Houk, Rose. *Wildflowers of the American West*. Chronicle Books, San Francisco, 1987.

Johnson, Olga W. *Flathead and Kootenay*. The Arthur H. Clark Company, Glendale, California, 1969.

Keen, Richard A. *Skywatch: The Western Weather Guide*. Fulcrum, Inc., Golden, Colorado, 1987.

Lavender, David. *The Rockies*. University of Nebraska Press, Lincoln, 1981.

Leopold, Aldo. *A Sand County Almanac*. Oxford University Press, New York, 1949.

McNulty, Tim. *Grand Teton National Park: Where Lightning Walks*. Woodlands Press, Del Mar, California, 1985.

_____. *Yellowstone National Park: Land of Fire and Falling Water*. Woodlands Press, Del Mar, California, 1986.

McPhee, John. *Rising from the Plains*. Farrar, Strauss & Giraux, New York, 1986.

Marschall, Mark C. *Yellowstone Trails: A Hiking Guide*. Yellowstone Library and Museum Association, Wyoming, 1984.

Marty, Sid. *Men for the Mountains*. Vanguard Press, New York, 1979.

Murie, Margaret and Olaus. *Wapiti Wilderness*. Colorado Associated University Press, Boulder, 1985.

Patton, Brian and Bart Robinson. *The Canadian Rockies Trail Guide*. Devil's Head Press, Canmore, 1978.

Russell, Andy. *Grizzly Country*. Alfred A. Knopf, New York, 1967.

_____. *Trails of a Wilderness Wanderer*. Alfred A. Knopf, New York, 1971.

Russell, Osborne. *Journal of a Trapper*. University of Nebraska Press, Lincoln, 1955.

Schmidt, Jeremy. *Adventuring in the Rockies*. Sierra Club Books, San Francisco, 1986.

Schullery, Paul. *Mountain Time*. Nick Lyons Books, New York, 1984.

_____. *The Bears of Yellowstone*. Roberts Rinehart, Boulder, 1986.

Stegner, Wallace. *Beyond the Hundredth Meridian*. Houghton Mifflin Company, Boston, 1954.

Tilden, Freeman. *The National Parks*. Ed. Paul Schullery. Alfred A. Knopf, New York, 1986.

U.S. Department of Agriculture. *When the Mountains Roared: Stories of the 1910 Fire*. Publication R1-78-30, Idaho Panhandle National Forests, Coeur d'Alene, Idaho.

Victor, Frances F. *River of the West*. R. W. Bliss and Company, Hartford, Connecticut, 1870.

Waidhofer, Linde. *High Color*. Western Eye Press, Telluride, Colorado, 1987.

Zwinger, Ann. *Beyond the Aspen Grove*. University of Arizona Press, Tucson, 1981.

_____. *Land Above the Trees*. University of Arizona Press, Tucson, 1989.

The Rockies was produced in association
with the publisher by McQuiston & Partners in
Del Mar, California: art direction, Don McQuiston;
editorial direction, Tom Chapman;
design and production supervision, Joyce Sweet;
mechanical production, Kristi Mendola;
map design and production, Patti Judd;
production coordination, Marci Wellens;
copyediting, Robin Witkin; composition, TypeLink;
text type, Goudy Old Style; printed and bound in
Japan by Dai Nippon Printing Company, Ltd.